This Is Where I Learned Of Love

CDCR 8/18/08 – 5/19/09

Jennifer Moon

Photographs by Patrick Connor

Collector's Edition

From *Phoenix Rising, Part 1: This Is Where I Learned Of Love*, 2012

ISBN: 978-1-300-58679-1

Originally printed © 2012 by Jennifer Moon as a limited edition of fourteen to accompany each photograph in the *Prison Relic* series

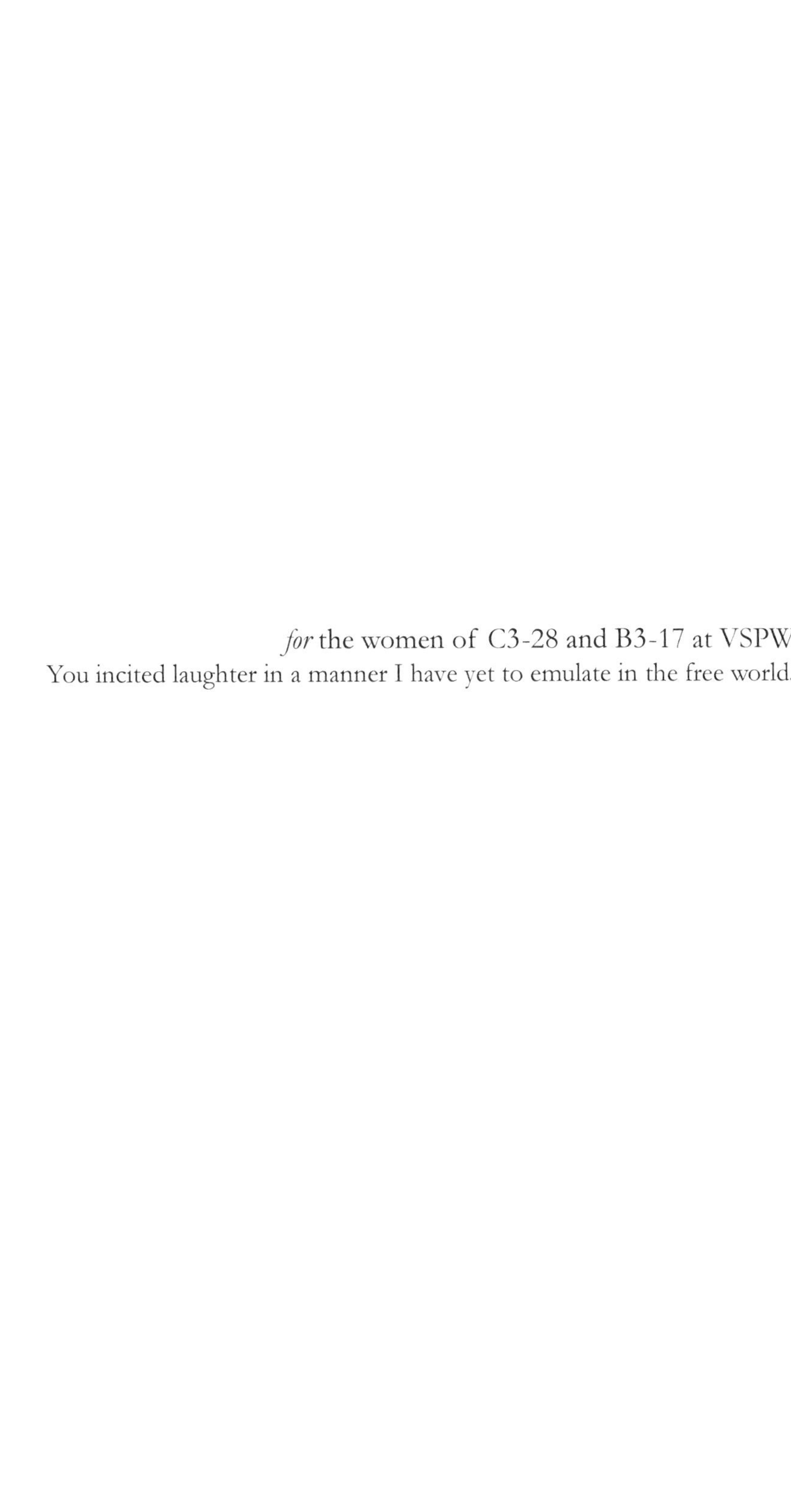

for the women of C3-28 and B3-17 at VSPW
You incited laughter in a manner I have yet to emulate in the free world.

Preface

On August 18, 2008 I was sentenced to eighteen months in state prison for attempted first-degree robbery.

Contents

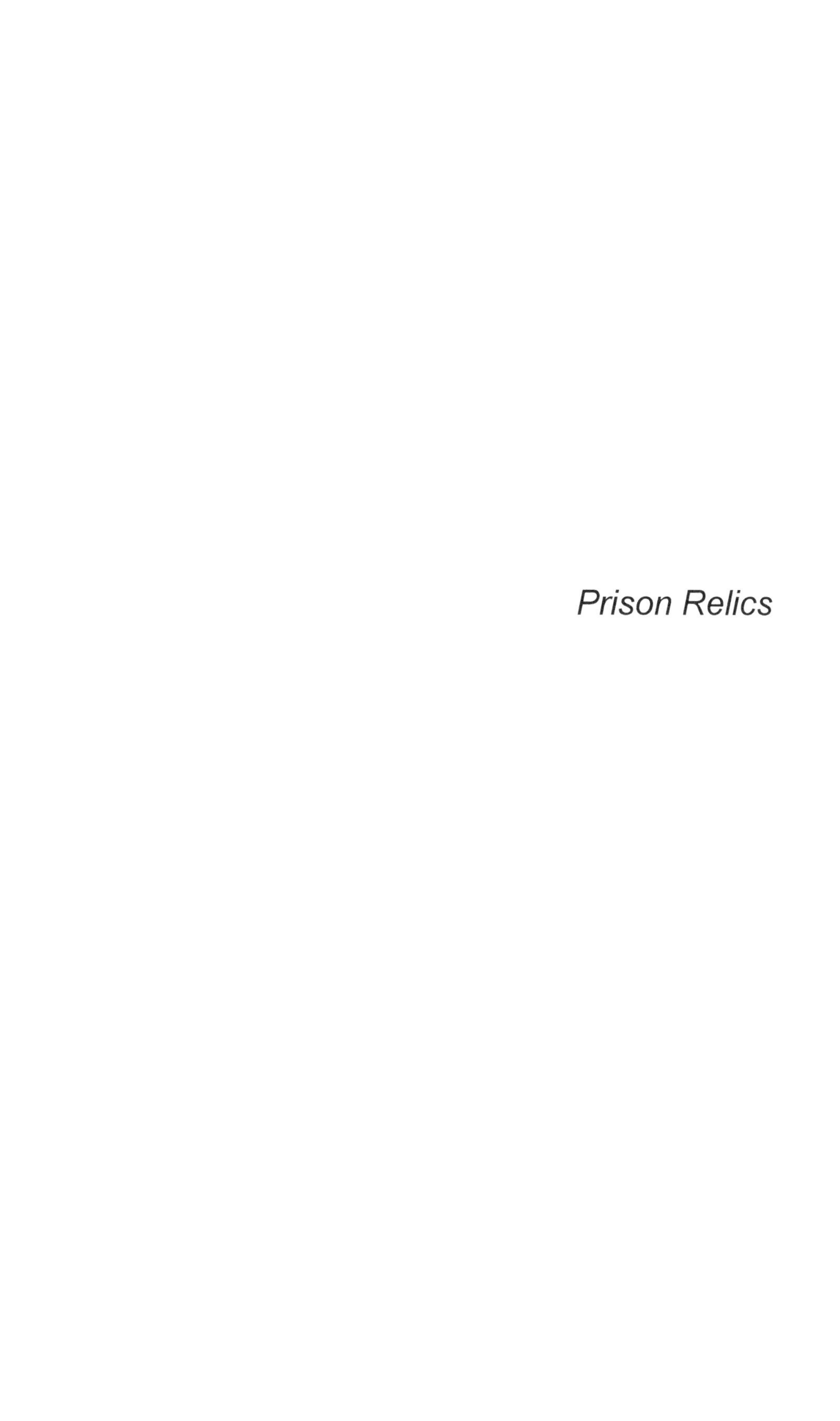

Prison Relics

CDC ID

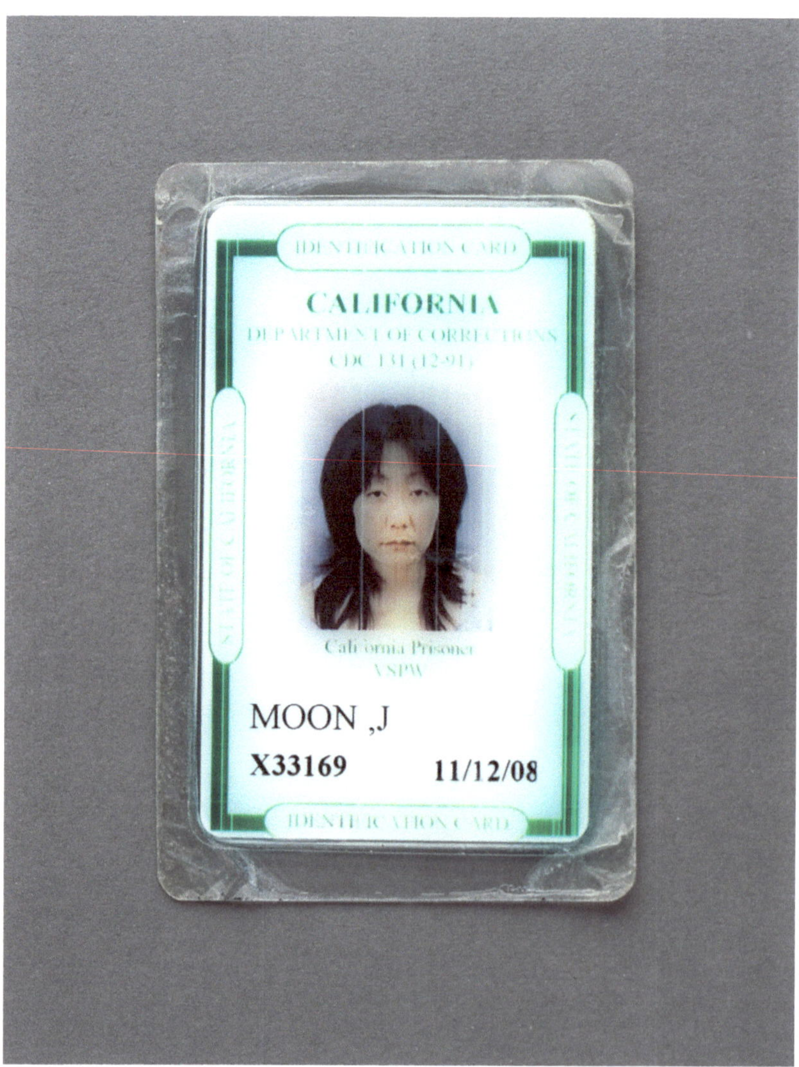

This is my CDC (California Department of Corrections) Identification Card for VSPW (Valley State Prison for Women), which is where I did the majority of my time. There are three female offender state correctional facilities in California. One is in Chino: CIW (California Institution for Women or "CI Wonderful" as some inmates affectionately refer to it), which is notable for housing the Manson Girls. The other two women's prisons are in Chowchilla. They are across the road from one another and are essentially identical in structure and design: CCWF (Central California Women's Facility) and VSPW. CCWF is generally known as the Southerner's prison and VSPW, the Northerner's, meaning new prisoners from Southern California do their Receiving (typically six weeks in RC or the Reception Center where incoming inmates are processed, evaluated, and classified) at CCWF and the Northerners do their Receiving at VSPW before "going over the wall" to their endorsed correctional facility, community correctional facility, Conservation (Fire) Camp or Alternative Custody Program. Death Row is housed at CCWF on A Yard, which is the same yard as RC. My first two weeks in prison, I lived in the unit next door to Death Row and I would watch, in transfixed awe, the condemned prisoners being steadily escorted to and from the chow hall in a single line.

CDC is responsible for the operation of California state prisons and parole systems. In 2004, it was renamed CDCR, California Department of Corrections and Rehabilitation, in response to a Corrections Independent Review Panel report listing a multitude of problems plaguing California's $6 billion correctional system, such as a recidivism rate far exceeding that of any other state (the recidivism rate at VSPW is approximately 72%), reported abuse of inmates by correctional officers, failure of correctional institutions to provide youth wards and inmates with mandated health care and other services, among other issues. CDCR is the second largest law enforcement or police agency in the United States (NYPD is listed as the country's largest while LAPD and LA County Sheriff's Department are listed as the fourth and fifth largest, respectively). The total inmate population from California's thirty-three adult correctional facilities, thirteen adult community correctional facilities and eight juvenile facilities makes CDCR the largest state-run prison system in the United States. The United States has the highest documented incarceration rate in the world. From 1920 to 2006, general U.S. population grew 2.8 times while the number of inmates increased more than 20 times. According to the U.S. Bureau of Justice Statistics, in 1980 the number of persons under correctional supervision (probation, jail, prison, or parole) was 1,840,400 (319,598 in prison). In 2009, the numbers escalated to 7,225,800 (1,524,513 in prison). I was one of the 1,524,523 in prison.

Typewriter

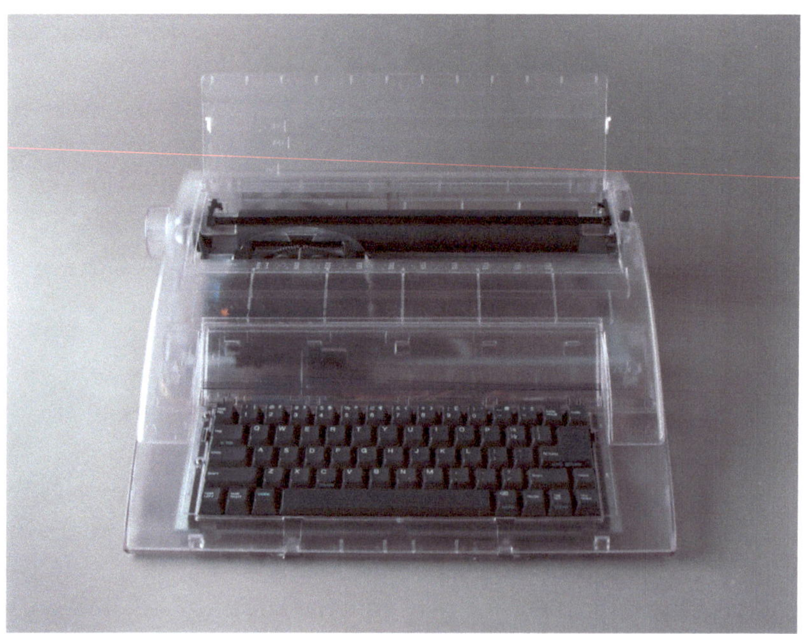

After leaving A Yard or "going over the wall" to your permanent location and once classified, inmates are allowed to receive Quarterly Packages and Special Purchases from state approved vendors. Quarterly Packages or "boxes" are limited to a maximum weight of 464 oz. per box and inmates may receive only one box per quarter (three months). Boxes commonly consist of popular brand-name hygiene products, personal clothing, and an exciting variety of food items not available at the prison canteen. They can also contain office products like a typewriter. Special Purchases are in addition to Quarterly Packages and are generally restricted to entertainment appliances, such as TV's and personal radio/CD players, electronic accessories (if purchased with an appliance), and musical instruments. Most prison appliances are clear to deter inmates from hiding contraband in them.

While my non-"indigent" fellow inmates were excited to get a TV, I eagerly anticipated my typewriter. I had this romantic and noble vision of political prisoners writing manifestos or other historically significant revolutionary material while imprisoned. Of course I was not a political prisoner, only a mere common criminal, but I fancied myself doing something glorious while in prison such as feverishly typing out The Manifesto for The Revolution while locked in a tiny cell, detained by a fascist administration. In reality, I primarily used my typewriter to hammer out exceedingly long letters to my former RP/L (Revolution Partner/Lover). Being my RP/L, we certainly discussed The Revolution but my letters were also significantly tainted by seemingly unquenchable insecurities and then later, dismay regarding his decision to end our RP/L relationship during my incarceration. In addition, I used my typewriter to create assignments for my Pseudo-Life Coaching Prison Project. My typewriter became a structural component of my prison identity: I set up a makeshift office in the dayroom using a broken ironing board as a desk. People would often come up to me and ask what I was working on and they would leave believing I was some encouraging perversion of a political prisoner.

Radio/CD Player with Headphones

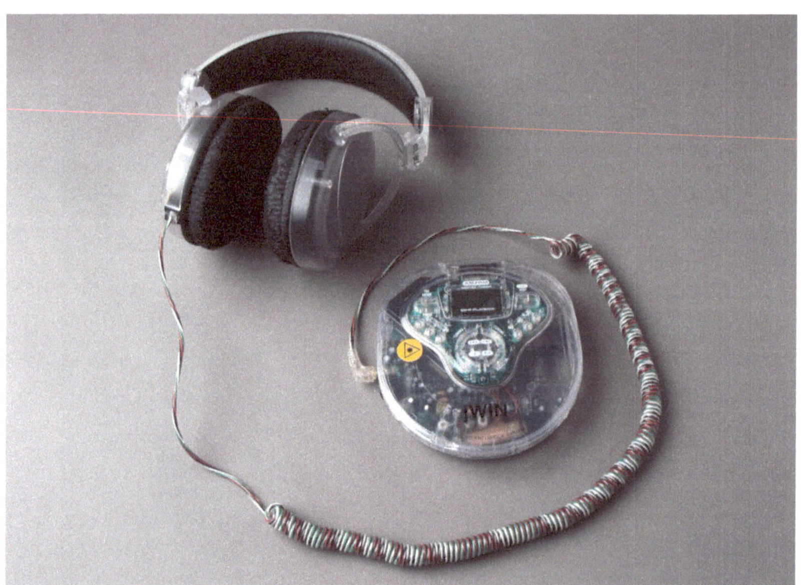

Having access to music is a huge asset in prison. Not only does music make an environment founded on confinement more bearable, it is invaluable to help sequester one from the loud arguments, dramas, and occasional violence that can easily erupt living in a cell with eight women. I can put on my headphones, crank up the music and pretend I'm somewhere else (and even made somewhat invisible) while one of my roommates dragged his girlfriend by the hair, punching her in the face as she scratched his. But prison is not always like that; there were many more fun times. It turned out getting the largest headphones available had another unexpected benefit: they can be flipped outward and made into speakers for a makeshift boom box. On occasions of lockdowns, we would often listen to music this way and play dominoes. And before I made friends, I would wear my headphones to and from the chow hall, especially in the very early mornings for breakfast, enthusiastically dancing along to the Cure's "Just Like Heaven" or, after my RP/L broke up with me, singing passionately to one of Bright Eyes' hyper-emotional songs. This also became one of my notable traits in prison.

Mini Light

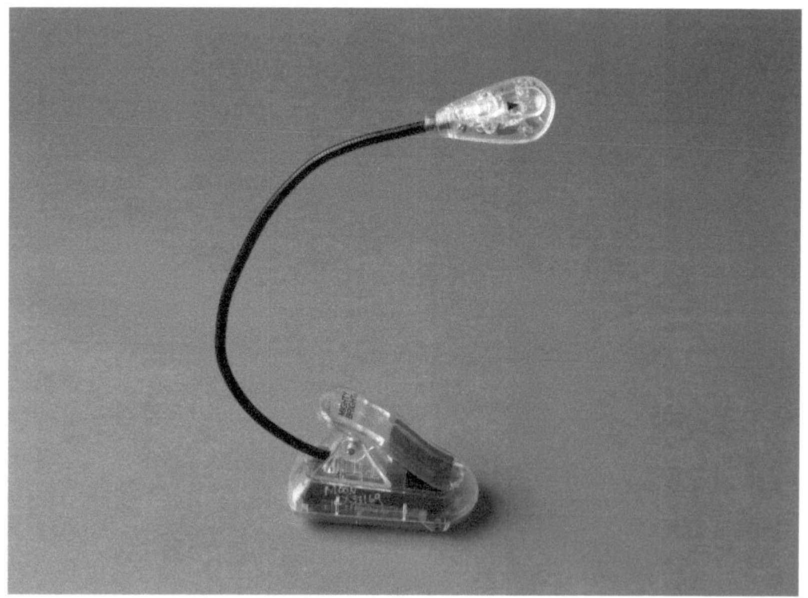

My reading light is truly a magic wand bringing forth light in darkness. One of the rooms I lived in would never turn on the bright light (except when required, like during count time) so it was challenging to read and write using only the dim light and especially in the lower bunk. Since I spent most of my downtime writing, this mini light became indispensable. Hunkered down in the shelter of my lower bunk, with my mini light creating a small glow in the darkness of the room, I almost felt like I was in a tent camping. And on a completely different note, my OCD-like behavior, which I had tendencies prior to prison, progressed during my incarceration. Many prisoners actually develop a fixation with cleanliness and enforce strict cleaning routines and rules, which vary in degree from room to room. My compulsion was largely isolated to hair and apparently this particular obsession is common. One room required all their occupants to wear their hair in braids or up in a bun to prevent loose hairs from falling onto the ground. Then there are the prison urban legends, which veteran prisoners love to tell the newbies on A Yard to scare them, one being of a girl whose hair accidentally fell onto her lower Bunkie's bed and her Bunkie proceeded to beat her in the head with a lock inside a pillow case. Whatever issue I had with control or loss of control or an attempt to maintain some semblance of control, I became hyper-vigilant about picking hair off my bed and pillow as well as off the floor and clothing (which continues to this day). Without fail, the first thing I would do every morning after Wake Up was to scan my bed for loose hairs using my mini light.

Cell Layout

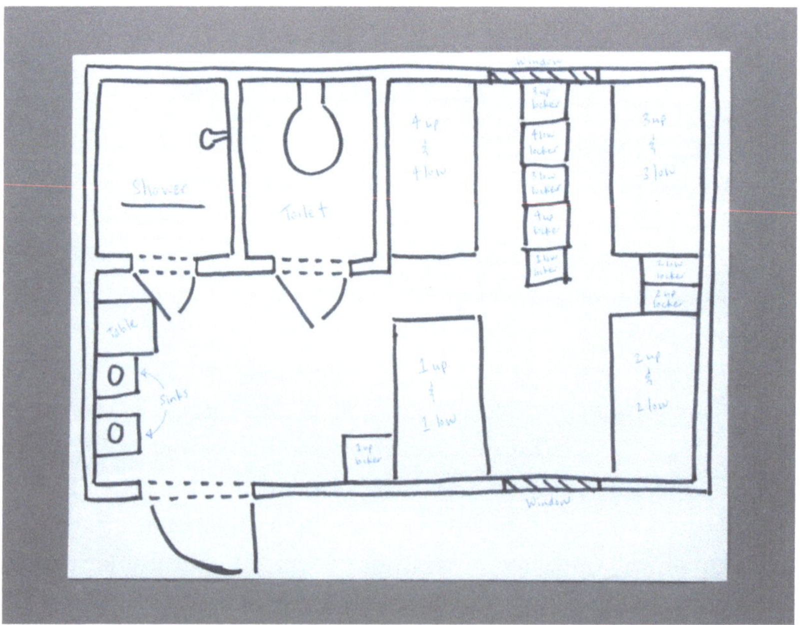

This is a rough blueprint of all the General Population rooms at both VSPW and CCWF. Each room is said to be 246 square feet and houses eight women with four bunk beds, eight tall lockers, a toilet, shower, two sinks with mirrors, and a movable table and chair. The toilet and shower have actual doors, which is nice to provide a notion of privacy: both doors have a huge, open hole cut out at the top and a smaller slit cut out at the bottom so the C.O.'s (Correctional Officers) can see who's in there and what you are doing. It's much better than the approximately 7' by 12' standard two-man cells where the toilet is out in the open and you have to shit or "boo-boo" right in front of your Bunkie. Also having a shower in your room is a major advantage because you can shower whenever you like as opposed to a two-man cell where you have to be let out of your cell and wait in line to take a hurried shower, which will not even happen if there's a lockdown. Some women who are in serious, romantic relationships may prefer the two-man cells for the privacy and to avoid dealing with so many "personalities," as they say. But I prefer the eight-man cells for the toilet and shower and also the significant difference in size compared to a two-man cell where really only one person can be off her bunk to occupy the short and narrow free space of the cell. I also enjoyed living with seven other women. It gave my stay a more community feel to it and I actually thought the varying "personalities" made it more fun or at least interesting. Of course, I was incredibly fortunate and never ended up in a scary, fascist room controlled by a dictator-like lifer (I've also met very kind and thoughtful lifers).

The best bunk in the room, if you are in a relationship like I was, is 3 Up and 3 Low. Beverly, my girlfriend, and I made a nice little home in our little corner. The lockers significantly limit the space (there's maybe two feet between the lockers and our bunk) but it also creates a wall and provides coverage. If you open 2 Low's and 1 Low's locker doors and if we are both on the lower bunk, we become virtually hidden from C.O.'s creeping down the hall looking through windows or popping doors and therefore avoid getting written up for "homosecting," as the C.O.'s call it, or "cupcaking," as the inmates refer to it. Homosexual activity is illegal in prison and can result in a 115 (rule violation write-up), time in the SHU (Security or Segregated Housing Unit), or separation of the couple if they live together (even to separate yards if they really want to be mean). Most regular-staff C.O.'s are generally aware of all the couples and the majority of them, unless they are obvious homophobes (like Radcliff, who threatened to write Bev and me up and take our Greens because we were talking too affectionately close out on the yard), don't care as long as you aren't "cupcaking" right in front of them. In fact, I had a few C.O.'s come up to Bev and me and say we were a cute couple. I personally believed we could have won Cutest Couple at VSPW if there was such a contest (or at least, Cutest Couple on B yard).

Beverly Photo

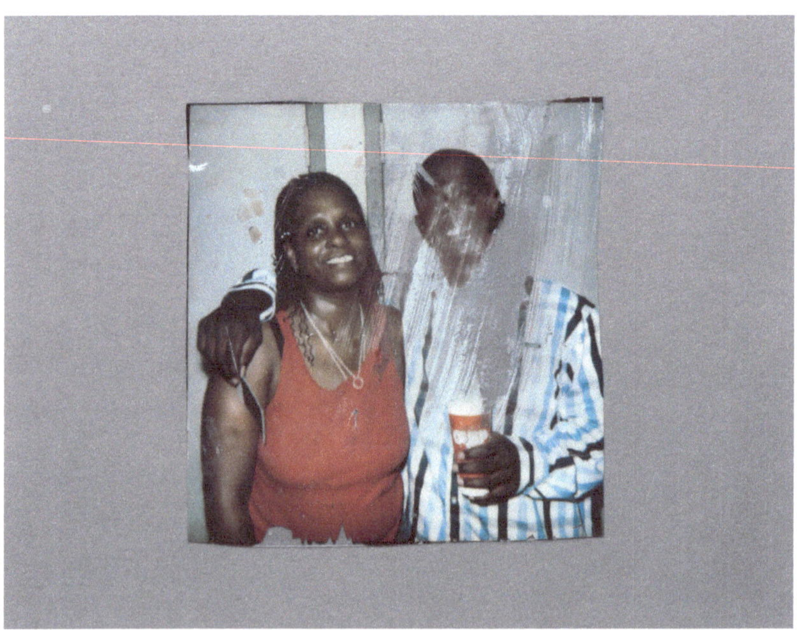

This photo of Beverly was the only one I had for a while after I paroled (I paroled five months before she did). I met Beverly when I moved into a Green room. Greens are inmates with gate passes who work outside the prison gates in one of the following job locations: almond farm, supply warehouse, utility warehouse, procurement, landscaping, garage/car wash, or Caltrans. They call workers with gate passes Greens because we have to wear fluorescent green outfits to work. All Greens are housed together down C hall in Unit 3 on B Yard. Beverly was an almond farmer and I was a clerk in the Procurement Office. About a month after my RP/L broke up with me, I became romantically involved with Beverly. We soon fell in love and she became my "honey," as they say in prison (no inmates use the term, girlfriend; you either have a honey or a wife). That's Beverly's eldest son next to her. The photo is fucked up and see-through in places because it's a Polaroid and we aren't allowed to have Polaroids (because you can hide drugs in between the layers) so when it was mailed to her, it was taken apart. Then Bev used indigent toothpaste (which also doubles as glue) to stick it to the underside of the top bunk above hers and when she tried to clean off the toothpaste, it also rubbed off the pigment of the photo.

Heart Locket Necklace

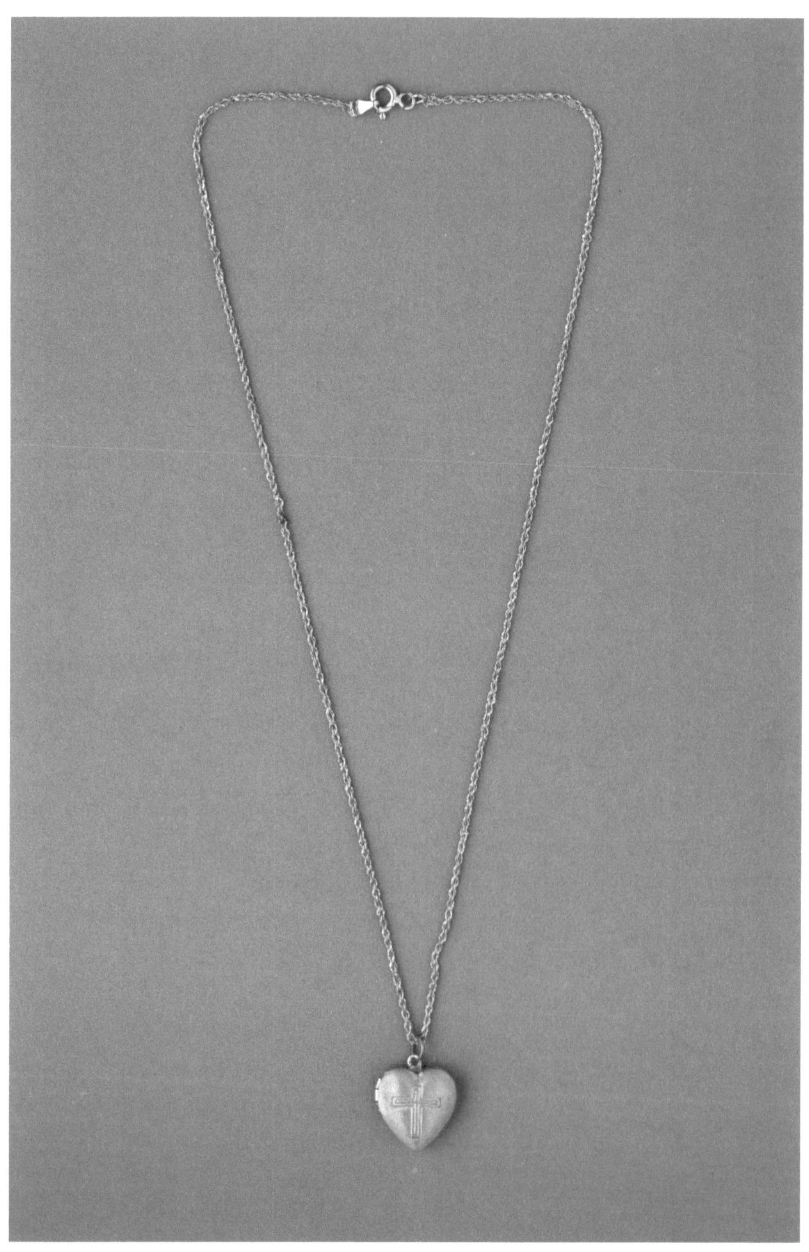

I believe this heart locket necklace is the only piece of jewelry I have ever received as a gift from a lover. Beverly bought it from one of the "crack heads," as she called them, for a $20 clavo (i.e., $20 worth of tobacco in prison). The tobacco trade in prison is analogous to drug dealing in the free world: many inmates will sell their canteen, box items, personal jewelry, even wedding rings for tobacco (similar to how addicts may behave with crack, for example). There are actual drugs in prison too, but that's an entirely different and more dangerous enterprise. I'm not fond of the term, "crack head," not only because I don't believe in name calling but because, before I got my Greens and became involved in tobacco trafficking myself, I certainly gave away much of my canteen and several highly anticipated box food items for $2-$4 (depending on who you are and what yard you are on) pinners, which they called cigarettes. This locket was making the rounds for Valentine's Day and Bev managed to buy it before anyone else (it looked a lot better and the locket used to be gold before I started showering with it). It has a cross on one side, which would generally deter me from wearing it, but Bev believes in that stuff and I love her, so I wore it backwards with the cross close to my heart because that's where Bev is. I kept a lock of Beverly's hair inside the locket.

Log

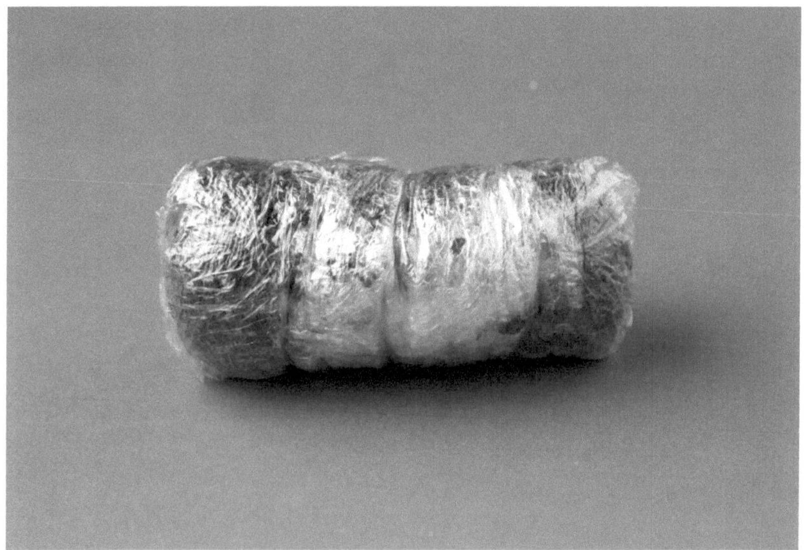

In 2005, California banned tobacco in all prisons. This inadvertently created an insanely profitable black market tobacco trade. Unlike smuggling illegal drugs into prison, which will catch you another criminal case, being caught with tobacco will generally result in a 115 (a rule violation write-up with the potential of losing 30-90 days) and if you work Greens, you loose your gate pass. The minor consequences have made trafficking tobacco more rampant and a more lucrative market than drugs. For example, the tobacco log depicted in the photo, which is approximately two pouches of tobacco, is about $250 (which can nearly double during times of drought).

Prison employees smuggle some of the tobacco in because, like the inmates, if they are caught, they may loose their jobs but rarely face criminal charges (and the temptation to make more money than their job pays can be difficult to pass up for some). However, the majority of tobacco and other contraband as well as illegal drugs are brought in by the Greens, specifically the farmers.

Despite their job title, farmers rarely farm or tend the orchard of almond trees. Instead their day generally consists of the following: deliveries or "hand-offs" of goods (e.g., tobacco); digging holes to bury the tobacco amongst the almond trees; climbing the trees to look out for C.O.'s patrolling the grounds; digging up tobacco and moving it to new locations; running and hiding from C.O.'s; keeping track of all the holes; separating the tobacco into logs; making log drop-offs to other Green locations for packers. Farmers became the chief traffickers of tobacco because they are the least supervised amongst all the Greens and they have the easiest access to free-world roads. The almond farm is large and some of its borders butt against open roads used by the free world. If you are a farmer, it is not uncommon to be approached by a lifer or long-timer in an attempt to set up a "hand-off," where a family member, friend, or lover of the lifer or long-timer will drive by the almond farm at a designated time and location to literally hand off a shipment of tobacco (or other contraband and the occasional drugs). Once the tobacco is separated into logs, the farmers drop-off the merchandise, usually in the trash bin near the garage/car wash and landscaping, to be distributed to designated packers who will then bring the logs into the institution. I was a clerk, which means I was able to walk around to the different locations in order to retrieve and deliver paperwork. So at one point (because the other clerk, who had been doing it for years, was now being watched), I acquired the job of transporting fifteen to twenty logs from the garage, strapped around my waist like a belt, to the warehouse so that those girls can get in on the action. Every five logs you successfully pack in, you get one log for yourself (which is an invaluable way to survive if you are indigent). And when I say pack, I mean inserted into your vagina or anus or both. Another element of working Greens is that at the end of every work day, you have to go through the process of being let back into the prison, which includes a full strip search: stripping down completely naked (even removing tampons), coughing and squatting three times simultaneously as a group, and then individually bending over, spreading your vagina and anus open using your hands while coughing as a C.O. shines a flashlight in you to catch any abnormalities. I've seen a few women get caught during the cough and squat (mostly coming out of the vagina, your asshole kinda sucks things into it once you get past a certain point).

Assignment #1

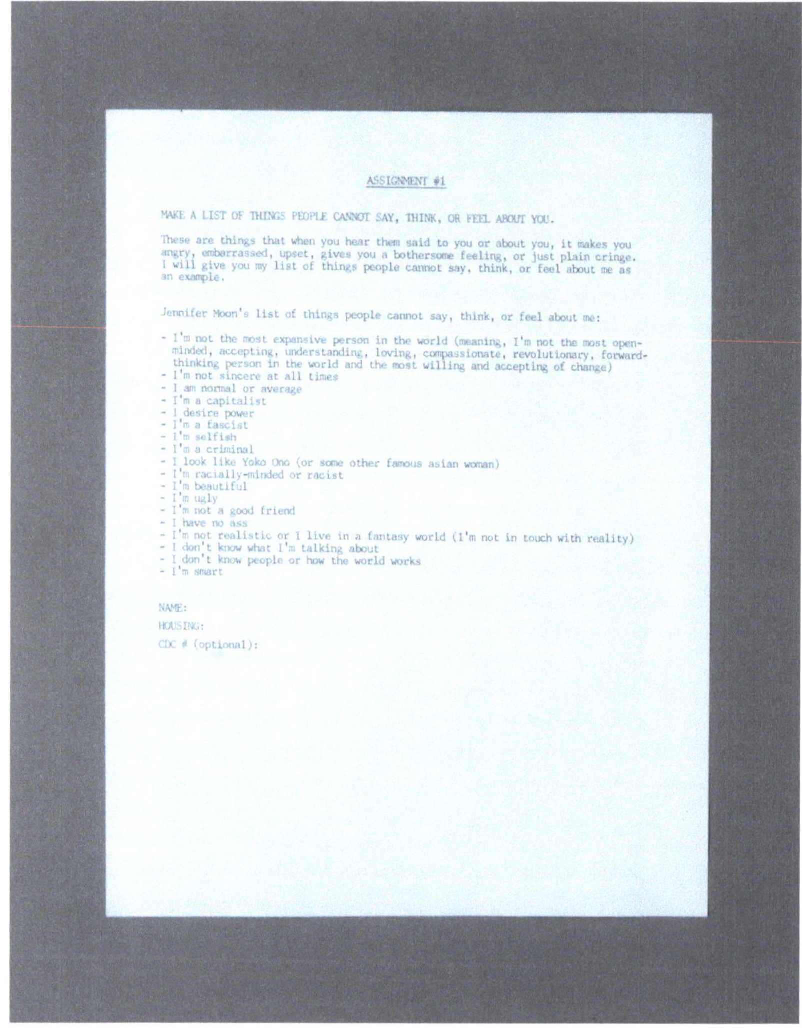

ASSIGNMENT #1

MAKE A LIST OF THINGS PEOPLE CANNOT SAY, THINK, OR FEEL ABOUT YOU.

These are things that when you hear them said to you or about you, it makes you angry, embarrassed, upset, gives you a bothersome feeling, or just plain cringe. I will give you my list of things people cannot say, think, or feel about me as an example.

Jennifer Moon's list of things people cannot say, think, or feel about me:

- I'm not the most expansive person in the world (meaning, I'm not the most open-minded, accepting, understanding, loving, compassionate, revolutionary, forward-thinking person in the world and the most willing and accepting of change)
- I'm not sincere at all times
- I am normal or average
- I'm a capitalist
- I desire power
- I'm a fascist
- I'm selfish
- I'm a criminal
- I look like Yoko Ono (or some other famous asian woman)
- I'm racially-minded or racist
- I'm beautiful
- I'm ugly
- I'm not a good friend
- I have no ass
- I'm not realistic or I live in a fantasy world (I'm not in touch with reality)
- I don't know what I'm talking about
- I don't know people or how the world works
- I'm smart

NAME:

HOUSING:

CDC # (optional):

Working Greens and living in a room with a lot of farmers and also having a girlfriend who was a farmer had its definite perks and advantages. Except during the rainy season, when the farmers wouldn't go to work sometimes for several days in a row, our room regularly had tobacco to smoke and for the most part we would share with one another. As a result of tobacco sales, we maintained a consistent supply of canteen and box food as well as hook-ups in the kitchen. Holding tobacco was akin to being a drug dealer. People treated you differently and I couldn't help but feel an enhanced sense of status and importance.

In an attempt to utilize my newfound resource and influence to stimulate some form of expansion and self-awareness, I started a Pseudo-Life Coaching Prison Project. This photo documents Assignment #1. In exchange for completion of Assignment #1, I would give a single cigarette. I borrowed the idea for Assignment #1 from my life coach friend, Michael Blomsterberg. Assignment #1 states "Make a list of things people cannot say, think, or feel about you. These are things that when you hear them said to you or about you, it makes you angry, embarrassed, upset, gives you a bothersome feeling, or just plain cringe." I found this exercise helpful to begin to uncover and identify beliefs, which unconsciously dictate my behavior and determine how I interact with others (e.g., my life centers on constantly trying to prove that I am none of the things I listed in the assignment, which then limits connection and a true, unrepressed awareness of others and the world). With the cigarette incentive, I managed to get over twenty participants. Assignment #2 was a one-on-one session to discuss Assignment #1. Only three or four people participated in Assignment #2 in exchange for a cigarette.

115

804 SENT TO RECORDS ON: 03-28-09 TABE: 12.9
CCCMS: NO
MH-115: NO

STATE OF CALIFORNIA — DEPARTMENT OF CORRECTIONS

RULES VIOLATION REPORT

CDC NUMBER	INMATE'S NAME	RELEASE/BOARD DATE	INST.	HOUSING NO.	LOG NO.
X-33169	MOON	3-20-09	VSPW	B3-17-04U	03-09-B-109

VIOLATED RULE NO(S).	SPECIFIC ACTS	LOCATION	DATE	TIME
3041(b)	REFUSING TO REPORT TO JOB ASSIGNMENT	PROCUREMENT OFFICE	03-26-09	0820

CIRCUMSTANCES

On Thursday, March 26, 2009 at approximately 1130 hours, while performing my duties as Officer Technician in the Procurement Office, I called Facility B3 Officer Zamora when INMATE MOON, X-33169, B3-17-04U, did not report for work. He found her in her room. I told Officer Zamora to send I/M MOON to work because there is nothing wrong with her, she just does not want to work. I/M MOON told Officer Zamora that she refuses to go to work. Officer Zamora relayed the message to me, and I told him that I was going to write her up for Refusal To Report To Work, and if he could inform I/M MOON. This is not the first time we have had an issue with I/M MOON and her desire to not work. I/M MOON was given a verbal warning earlier this month when I saw I/M MOON with her head on her desk and I returned to the office at approximately 1100 hours, I told her that she cannot lay her head on her desk. She said she didn't care if she was written up, I/M MOON just wanted to go back to her room to continue typing her "Manifesto" for the revolution she is planning. My supervisor, B. Sanders PSOII, called I/M MOON and myself into her office. We discussed with I/M MOON the importance of staying with the program since she is a short-timer. I/M MOON agreed to stay and was not written up that day. I request that I/M MOON be sent to classification at the earliest possible time to be removed from this work assignment. I/M MOON is aware of this report. I/M MOON **IS NOT** a patient/participant in the Mental Health Delivery System. I/M MOON **IS NOT** a part of the Disability Placement and/or Developmentally Disabled Program.

REPORTING EMPLOYEE (Typed Name and Signature)	DATE	ASSIGNMENT	RDO'S
▶ T. HEFLER, OFFICER TECHNICIAN	3/26/09	PROCUREMENT OFFICE	S/S/H

REVIEWING SUPERVISOR'S SIGNATURE	DATE	INMATE SEGREGATED PENDING HEARING
▶ B SANDERS, PSOII	3/27/09	N/A DATE LOC N/A

CLASSIFIED	OFFENSE DIVISION	DATE	CLASSIFIED BY (Typed Name and Signature)	HEARING REFERRED TO
☐ ADMINISTRATIVE ☑ SERIOUS	[illegible]	[illegible]	▶ [illegible]	☐ HO ☑ SHO ☐ SC ☐ FC

COPIES GIVEN INMATE BEFORE HEARING

☑ CDC 115	BY (STAFF'S SIGNATURE)	DATE	TIME	TITLE OF SUPPLEMENT		
	▶ [signature]	3-30-09	2030	N/A		
☐ INCIDENT REPORT LOG NUMBER	BY (STAFF'S SIGNATURE)	DATE	TIME	BY (STAFF'S SIGNATURE)	DATE	TIME
N/A	▶ N/A			▶ N/A		

HEARING

HEARING PREPARATION:

On April 2, 2009, at 1955 hours, INMATE (I/M) MOON, X-33169 made a personal appearance before this Senior Hearing Officer. She acknowledged she was in good health and ready to proceed with the hearing at this time. The subject was advised of the charges against her and the purpose of this hearing.

MENTAL HEALTH SERVICES DELIVERY SYSTEM:

According to mental health records, I/M MOON **IS NOT** a participant in the Mental Health Services Delivery System (MHSDS). The behavior resulting in the RVR was not considered bizarre, unusual or uncharacteristic, therefore did not warrant the completion of a CDC 115-MH.

DUE PROCESS TIME CONTRAINTS:

This disciplinary was served on the inmate within 15 days of discovery. All time constraints have been met. There are no due process issues.

REFERRED TO ☐ CLASSIFICATION ☐ BPT/NAEA

ACTION BY (TYPED NAME)		SIGNATURE	DATE	TIME
A. FURBERT, CORRECTIONAL LIEUTENANT		▶ [signature]	4/2/09	1955 HRS
REVIEWED BY (SIGNATURE)	DATE	CHIEF DISCIPLINARY OFFICER'S SIGNATURE	DATE	
▶ D. PENNER, FACILITY B CAPTAIN	4/3/09	▶ R. PADILLA, CDO	[illegible]	
☑ COPY OF CDC 115 GIVEN INMATE AFTER HEARING		BY (STAFF'S SIGNATURE) ▶ [signature]	[illegible]	[illegible]

CDC 115 (7/88)

A 115 is a disciplinary report that can result in a loss of 30-90 days (or more depending on the seriousness of the violation), which means your parole date gets moved back. This was the only 115 I ever received and it was for a refusal to report to work. I claimed I was sick, which still requires me to go through the process of reporting to work in order to get a ducat from my work supervisor to go to medical, then return back into the prison, which requires the usual strip search, cough & squat ordeal, and finally reporting to medical in order to receive another ducat to excuse me from work (if I were really sick, this entire process, which could take hours, would be daunting and I'd probably still opt for the write-up instead). In reality, I was not sick that day. I wanted to stay home with Beverly because she had just lost her Greens, not for tobacco but for horsing around while waiting to be let out of the prison for work. She attempted to throw an empty vitamin bottle full of rocks over the double, electric fence of the prison perimeter to see if she could do it (and on the coaxing of her fellow farmers). It landed in the space between the two fences and the C.O.'s had to fish it out without getting electrocuted. This act was considered a security risk, which cost Beverly her gate pass (or more importantly, her position in the tobacco trade).

I find my 115, for a simple refusal to report to work, both incredibly delightful and absurdly ridiculous because of the highlighted portion, which reads, "She said she didn't care if she was written up, I/M MOON just wanted to go back to her room to continue typing her "Manifesto" for the revolution she is planning." During my incarceration, I had a penchant for calling C.O.'s and free-staff fascists if they exhibited any enamoration of power or oppressive behavior. I found this to be an unexpected and continual source of entertainment because I would get varying responses from confusion mixed with uncertainty on how to respond to exclaiming, "What did you call me?!!" and sometimes the occasional laughter. In addition, I was a bit of a smart-ass at work with some of the free-staff in the both the Procurement Office and Supply Warehouse Office. So when I refused to report to work, these disgruntled free-staff seized the opportunity to get me reassigned by attempting to portray me as unstable or inherently insubordinate because of my commitment to revolution. During my hearing, the lieutenant, without even referencing what was written in the report, dropped it down to a 128, which is just a warning, and I remained a clerk in the Procurement Office until I paroled.

Birthday Card

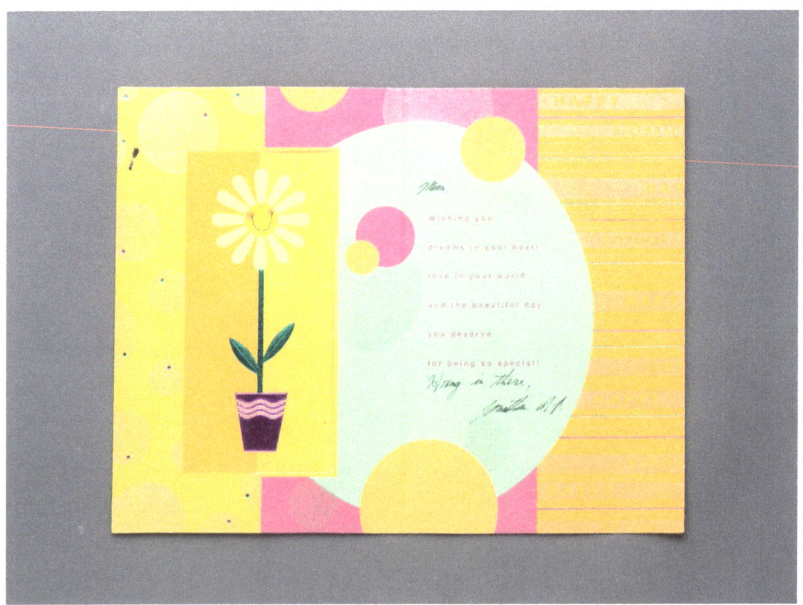

This is a birthday card from my former RP/L (Revolution Partner/Lover). At this point we were no longer RP/L's, just R.P.'s (as his signature suffix indicates). I certainly appreciate his thoughtfulness and wholeheartedly agree with the sentiment expressed in the card: embracing dreams, love, and beauty in my heart, world, and day. A friend once told me that whenever he hears the catchphrase, "hang in there," he imagines that poster of a cat grasping on for dear life, dangling off a tree branch. Now I always imagine the same thing. I'm not sure I would have the capacity to dream, love, or recognize beauty if all I can do is "hang in there."

Valentine Card

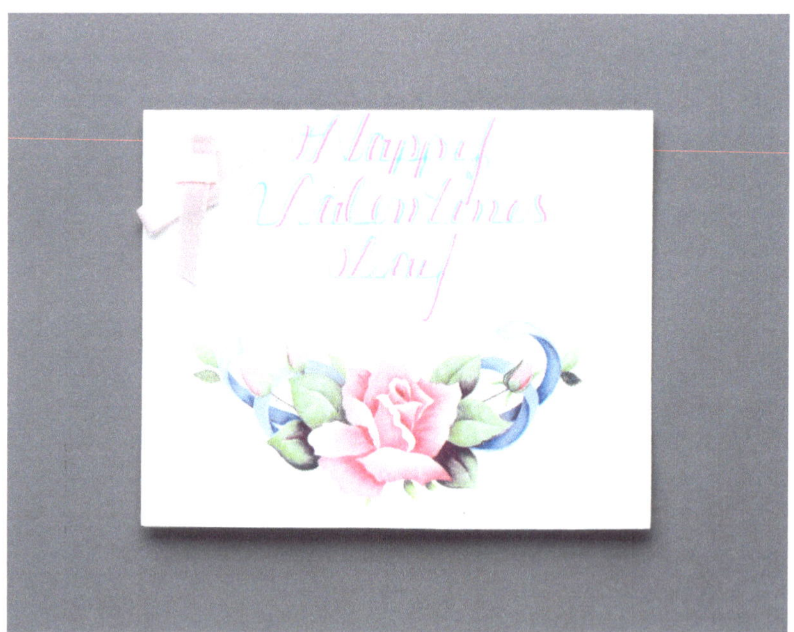

This is a Valentine's Day card from Beverly, which she bought from one of the inmate artists on our yard. I love prison art for its simultaneous crudeness as a result of the limited resources and the exquisite care and tenderness it embodies being made by someone who fully immerses herself in her craft because she has nothing but time. This one is especially lovely, I think.

Watch

ACTION
QUARTZ
LONDON
RIO - 4
PAR+1
NYK
5
BKK
+7
MSW
+3
HR
MIN
PLAY
CALENDAR
AUTO
MODE
SET
QUARTZ

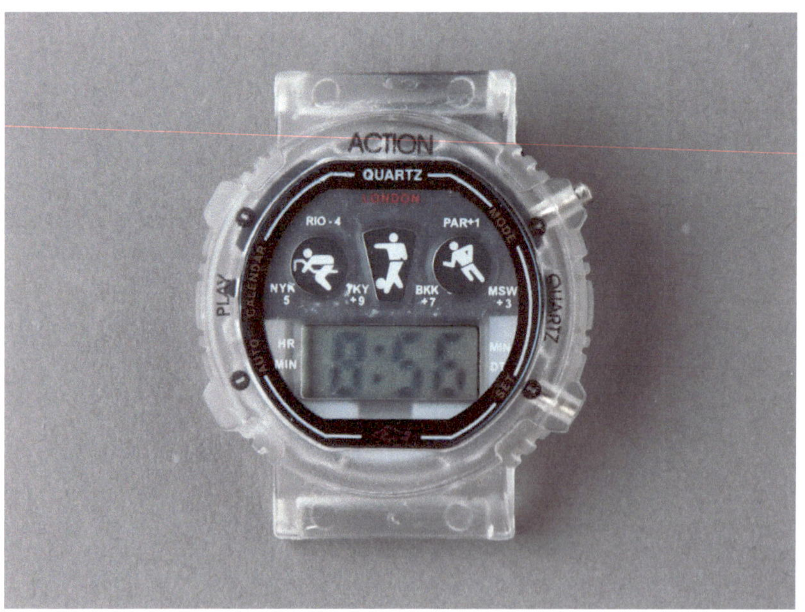

When I received my very first box (Quarterly Package), a few of my roommates asked why I got a watch. At the time, I didn't understand why this perplexed them or why they seemed to disapprove. Now I understand. The notion of time is probably the most oppressive aspect of incarceration. There are only two occasions when prisoners fixate on time (unless, of course, you are a lifer). The first occasion is after you meet with your counselor in RC and receive your "Face Sheet," which calculates your parole date. Almost everyone, including myself, spends the rest of the day recalculating the time, which begins with the amount of time you were sentenced minus half time or 85% and minus any good time/work time credits you might have received from county jail. And almost everyone, including myself, believes her time has been miscalculated. The second occasion is when inmates approach their parole date. They will say, "I have 31 days and a wake-up," "30 days and a wake-up," "29 days and a wake-up," etc., etc. (and this can begin as early as three or four months prior to their parole date). Other than these two occasions, prisoners do not want to hear about time or be made aware of it by wearing a watch or having a clock constantly in their site (there are no clocks in the cells). There really is no need for clocks anyway: scheduled unlocks for chow, work/school release, meds, and yard/dayroom determine the time. It was only during extended lockdowns that my roommates would occasionally ask me what time it is. Interestingly enough, the prison atmosphere must have rejected my watch because the wristbands suddenly broke off a week or two after I got it.

Since I was a short-timer or "just passing through," as they say, my relationship to time probably wasn't as oppressive or daunting as it is to many of my fellow inmates. Though it was certainly enough to cause me significant grief when I first heard my sentence and while I sat in jail waiting to "catch the chain." Anticipating the nightmarish notion of the sameness of time was almost unbearable and I imagined this hellish sameness would slow time down to a painful crawl. "Everyday is the same" is a common prison motto. However, much to my surprise, time actually passed rather quickly in prison. Perhaps it was because I was only "passing through" or maybe it was because I was engaged in a prison romance or maybe the regimentation and sameness actually makes time move faster. Whatever the case may be, when asking other inmates who had been there for years, they generally had a similar response: it went quickly. Ever since, my understanding and relationship to time has forever shifted. I think it's more the idea of time that is unsettling. As they say in prison, "You do the time, don't let the time do you."

Certificate of Discharge

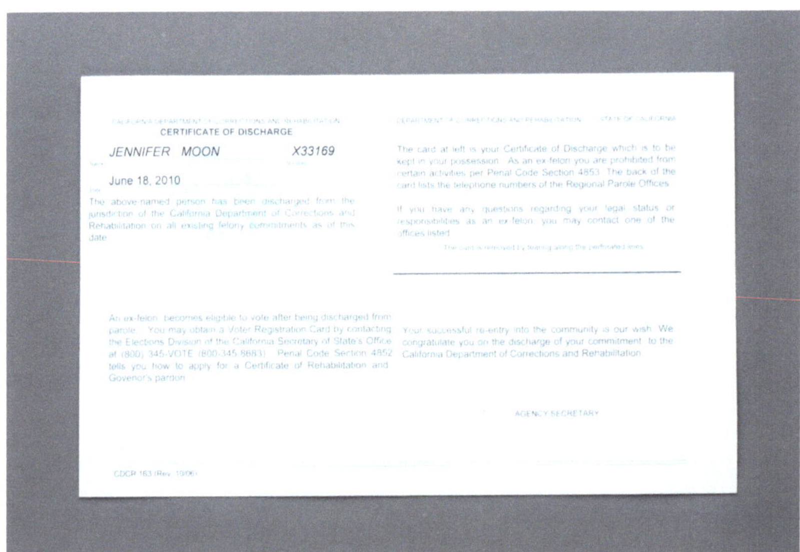

CALIFORNIA DEPARTMENT OF CORRECTIONS AND REHABILITATION

CERTIFICATE OF DISCHARGE

JENNIFER MOON X33169

June 18, 2010

The above-named person has been discharged from the jurisdiction of the California Department of Corrections and Rehabilitation on all existing felony commitments as of this date

DEPARTMENT OF CORRECTIONS AND REHABILITATION STATE OF CALIFORNIA

The card at left is your Certificate of Discharge which is to be kept in your possession. As an ex-felon you are prohibited from certain activities per Penal Code Section 4853. The back of the card lists the telephone numbers of the Regional Parole Offices.

If you have any questions regarding your legal status or responsibilities as an ex-felon, you may contact one of the offices listed.

The card is removed by tearing along the perforated lines.

An ex-felon becomes eligible to vote after being discharged from parole. You may obtain a Voter Registration Card by contacting the Elections Division of the California Secretary of State's Office at (800) 345-VOTE (800-345-8683). Penal Code Section 4852 tells you how to apply for a Certificate of Rehabilitation and Govenor's pardon.

Your successful re-entry into the community is our wish. We congratulate you on the discharge of your commitment to the California Department of Corrections and Rehabilitation.

AGENCY SECRETARY

CDCR 163 (Rev. 10/06)

Parole is defined as "the release of a prisoner temporarily (for a special purpose) or permanently before the completion of a sentence, on the promise of good behavior" (New Oxford American Dictionary, 2nd edition). Non-violent offenders, without prior strike(s), serve 50% of their sentence in a correctional facility. Violent offenders or offenders with prior strike(s) serve 85%. Once released back into the community, offenders remain under the jurisdiction of the California Department of Corrections and Rehabilitation as parolees to carry out the remainder of their sentence. The following is an incomplete list of standard Conditions of Parole and does not include any Special Conditions:

- The parolee, their residence, and possessions can be searched at any time of the day or night, with or without a warrant, and with or without a reason.

- Parolees are obligated to tell their parole agent about a new address before they move.
- Parolees are obligated to tell their parole agent, within three days, if they get a new job.
- Parolees are obligated to obtain permission from their parole agent to travel more than 50 miles from their residence.
- Parolees are obligated to receive a travel pass before they leave the county for more than two days.
- Parolees are obligated to receive a travel pass before they can leave the State.
- Parolees are obligated to tell their parole agent immediately if they get arrested or get a ticket.
- Parolees are obligated to not be around guns, or things that look like a real gun, bullets, or any other weapons.
- Parolees are obligated to not have a knife with a blade longer than two inches, except a kitchen knife. Kitchen knives must be kept in your kitchen.
- Parolees are obligated to report to their parole agent when told to report or a warrant can be issued for their arrest.
- Parolees are obligated to follow their parole agent's instructions.
- If a parolee breaks the law, they can be sent back to prison even if they do not have any new criminal charges.

The average length of parole is three years, though some can be five or ten years, depending on the crime, and life long parole supervision for those convicted of murder. For most non-violent offenders there is a possibility of early discharge from parole after twelve months of disciplinary free parole supervision and becomes effective after the thirteenth month. For violent and/or serious offenders within the average parole term of three years, the normal discharge review is after twenty-four months of continuous parole and becomes effective after the twenty-fifth month.

Once you complete your commitment to the California Department of Corrections and Rehabilitation, you receive a Certificate of Discharge that congratulates you on your successful re-entry into the community and informs you that you are now eligible to vote and that, as an ex-felon, you are prohibited from certain activities.

Excerpts from *"Dear RP/L…"*:
a story of love, revolution, and freedom (and lack thereof)

Part I: Waiting to Catch the Chain

"There's one more thing I'd really like for you to do.
Never leave me alone."
– Nate Dogg

CRDF (Century Regional Detention Facility), Lynwood, CA

8/20/08

Dearest Jonathan: My RPL, My Sweetest, Most Loved & Loving, Expansive, Sexiest Boy,

I just tried calling you but I guess there's no more money on your account—I called twice more just to make sure it wasn't all confused like last time. So I'm writing you a letter instead. I hope you're doing well. I'm doing much better today. After I talked to you yesterday in the early evening, I got moved to one of the prison modules where I'm gonna be housed permanently until I leave for prison (which may not be for two to three weeks according to fellow prisoners—you can actually check yourself on that website under my status: when it says "SP4" that means I'm about to go). I'm in 3700 (cell 21), which is the same module as I was in 5 ½ months ago and, unfortunately, some of the same girls are still here—a few of them have already come up to me saying, "Hey weren't you just here?" The difference between temporary housing and permanent housing is so significant for me, not only because I have access to books, paper, pencils, commissary […] but the move has also helped me psychologically and emotionally. There's something very dark and depressing about temporary housing, plus it's unbearably freezing in the cells. Permanent housing […] is much warmer (temp wise as well as atmosphere)—the dayroom is much larger and it's carpeted, the girls seem more relaxed and friendlier.

So I totally tagged my cell wall, next to my bunk (which is the top bunk). I'm totally proud of them and I think they'll stay for a long time 'cause they're small. I basically wrote the same slogans we tagged in Westwood (I also quoted two BRMC lyrics: "suicide's easy, what happened to the revolution" & "I won't waste my love on a nation") but I wrote out the full name of each faction after each anagram (is that what it's called?) so I think it looks and reads way cooler (also because it's in a jail cell—or maybe that just makes it sad and pathetic). […] So we have ODAP (Organization for the Dis-enamorment ~~with~~ of [I think 'of' is better, esp. after reading Foucault preface] Authoritative Power), IRFU (Institute for the Restructuring of the Family Unit)—by the way, I rethought it and I think "restructuring" is better than "regeneration" 'cause the latter made me think of reviving (what do you think?)—and PECDO (Peaceful Economic transition to Collective Dis-Ownership), etc., and then I quoted BRMC and wrote BRMC (Black Rebel Motorcycle Club). I thought it was a bit humorous but maybe it just seems funny to me because I've been re-reading and looking at my tags for the past three or four hours.

The other exciting thing that happened today was I went to a three-hour parenting class just to get the fuck out of my cell; but it actually turned out to be kind of fun and expansive, and definitely a venue for me to begin establishing myself as a revolutionary icon among my fellow prisoners. [...] So the parenting class was really more of a self-love class. The readings and exercise were extremely reminiscent of reading/exercises we'd do in Michael's group or Janet's group at Friendly House. [...] So if you look at the exercise sheet, it's titled, "Twenty Things You Love To Do!," and I of course took the exercise very seriously. The instructor wanted each of us to volunteer one of the things on our list. Most girls said usual things: shopping, sex, eating, etc.; and then some slightly unusual things: gang banging and "functioning" (which is some specific and more intense way to socialize); and then I raise my hand and say the first thing on my list, "plan & execute the revolution to destroy capitalism and other oppressive systems." The whole room quieted for a second, while some of the girls closest to me were like "right on" and gave me high fives. The rest of the room didn't hear me so they asked me to repeat it a couple of times. The best part was when one of the girls at the far tables yelled out, "Is that why you're here?" I just looked at her and smiled because how friken cool would it be if I was going to prison for a revolutionary cause rather than a stupid attempted robbery! Not to be racial, but it may be interesting to note that the african-americans seemed to be the most interested in the things I was saying (which is actually not that surprising given their history and struggles regarding socio-political issues); yet since they already are invested somewhat in revolt or opposition to the established order, many of them also behave in a reactionary manner rather than in an expansive way (I'm being very vague about his because I don't want to fall into stereotyping or any type of categorizing—perhaps I shouldn't have started this discussion, but do you know what I'm talking about?). The last issue I want to bring up is in regards to the word, "expansion." The instructor went over 9 needs of all humans (I listed them, or at least most of them, at the end of the two-page "Self-Care" document). Well #9 is Expansion; and when I heard that I couldn't help but exclaim aloud, "What?! I cannot believe you are using that word!" (at this point, my minimal outburst didn't seem too unusual because I've already made deliberate yet careful and not-too-obnoxious commentary throughout the class). Yet she used "expansion" to mean physical or literal expansion, as in having a child to expand a part of you to the next generation (this is a parenting class so I guess that interpretation makes sense); and this use of the word is extremely problematic to me as I know it is to you 'cause you mentioned a similar concern early on in our relationship. What are other words for "expansion"? Although I still really like the word so...

Now to move onto my newest obsession, which is most definitely brought on by situational circumstance yet also definitely subsiding as my acceptance level increases, and that is our relationship and you... Our current situation can actually be used to further romanticize our relationship: one of us, namely me, ends up going to prison = tragic romance due to forced separation by punitive law (i.e., one of the oppressive systems we're fighting to expand; and by the way, Commissioner Rose did send me to prison for purely punitive reasons—he made it clear during my sentencing that his job and the court's job is not to offer option of recovery for a defendant but to punish her/him and that's what he did—and I don't know about you but I will always favor options of recovery to pure punishment for punishment sake). So I view this whole tragically romantic scenario as somewhat of a test of our love for one another, a test of our expansive/formless relationship, and a test of our commitment to the revolution that one of the systems we're fighting to change is the very thing keeping us apart. Shit, this is all good stuff for a revolution/love song, don't you think? Do you feel similarly at all or is it just me? Please tell me your thoughts regarding me and our relationship 'cause I hate when I start speculating (and it's ok if you feel you may be repeating yourself—at this point I need reassurance so please just indulge me for the time being). Thank you!

So even though I may need to hear shit from you to reassure me of your love and commitment to me, I also do truly trust in our sincere and deep love for one another. I know you love me dearly because I've felt it when we were together physically. As I mentioned on the phone and not to be too transparently arrogant, but I know it will be hard for you to find someone as kind, easy-going, sincere, open, aware, thoughtful, revolutionary, and striving to continuously expand as me. And if you do, she probably won't be as cute, charming, and charismatic as me :). But if you do happen to find someone who possesses all the expansive traits listed above and who is also way hotter than me, then I say touché and fucking go for it (but I hope you would still help with the revolution). So knowing the improbability of you finding someone of my caliber or more to share your affections with, my only concern is that you may just not be capable of giving me what I need—all this may simply be too hard for you (and once again I sincerely apologize for not being there for you, to support you, during a time when you're going to experience significant change and growth—going to MI, living on your own, expanding your musical endeavors, etc.—and I am truly sad that I will not be there physically to share your expansion). I remember thinking after our very first phone conversation, after I got taken away, that you may not be capable of providing me with the words I need to feel supported and loved because you may not be capable of enduring the pain and heartache you'll most likely feel, off and on, being forced to love me from afar and wait for me. For me, those ideas can be highly romantic and I can feed off of that for quite some time. But for you, if the pain is too great or the relationship becomes too difficult or too complex or for the simple fact that I won't be physically around, you may not be able to help yourself, your feelings for me may inadvertently subside or dissipate without you really wanting them to, yet they do simply as a coping mechanism. Does this make sense? Do you feel this way? Or am I reading too much into things as usual? Please be honest with me because as I've stressed on numerous occasions, honesty-no-matter-what is of utmost importance if we are to remain on the expansive path.

So all of this is to somewhat lead up to my concern of your potential loneliness, especially living alone. I know for me, loneliness is one of my most significant triggers. Perhaps it's not so much for you. But if it is, I'd rather you not be lonely and therefore potentially trigger you to use; so if you must get an interim/temporary girlfriend, just make sure she is fully aware from the beginning that you're heart belongs to me (unless of course it no longer does or never did, in which case please tell me so I no longer delude myself). Just tell her that your girlfriend or your RPL (I really like this anagram [*sic*]—could be a good title for a song?) is doing some hard time in the Pen and when I get out, she'd better skedaddle or else I'll kick her ass—you know I'm completely joking. I would actually feel sorry for the poor girl because how could she not fall in love with you :). Ok, I know I'm totally speculating and hopefully this won't happen but if it does, this would definitely be a situation which calls for full disclosure of your relationship with this other currently imaginary broad—I mean I would want a day-to-day, hour-to-hour if need be, account of the development of your relationship. You understand why this particular situation would be pertinent to my full disclosure request I've stated in the beginning of our relationship, right? Well, seeing as the only reason we're not together is because I'm forced to go to prison—it wasn't a decision either one of us made—then it seems especially appropriate that you provide me details of your optional, wholly speculative, and hopefully remaining imaginary relationship with an interim girlfriend so as to maintain the intense level of intimacy and trust in our relationship. Do you concur, my darling? I love you! Sorry I'm being so heavy but I need to get this out and know that you understand how I feel and what I expect or desire and also hopefully get feedback from you about where you're at, how you feel about us, our relationship, and what your expectations or desires are of me and our relationship. I'm hoping and assuming that nothing's really changed between us, except for the obvious forced separation. But please tell me if it has or even if your feelings haven't changed 'cause I wanna hear it anyways just so I have something to hold onto here in my severe isolation. Once again, thank you for indulging me—it means more to me than I would have ever expected (it's amazing how the simple words, "I will wait for you," can carry me through severe and harsh feelings and times of isolation and loneliness—but if you truly don't mean it, please don't say it; yet I ask that you at least explain why [I really don't mean to pressure you: please just try to understand that I do feel waves of desperation at times but that it's purely situational]).

[…] Wow, I really miss you right now. What I wouldn't do to just hold you, feel your body pressed close against mine. I really cherish the last day and nights we spent together: planning the revolution in a hookah bar, taggin' Westwood, sharing affections, love and sex, falling asleep in your warm embrace, our naked bodies entwined throughout the night, waking up in your arms, smiling at me, grabbing my waist and pulling my body back up against yours while affectionately asking, "Where you going, baby?" (by the way, I love it when you call me 'baby'), spending the whole entire day and night with you, and then Sat night after hearing you perform at the musician's meeting lying in your bed, cuddling and talking enthusiastically, and then making love... I think very fondly of our last night together, not only because it happened to be the last time we're going to be able to be physically intimate like that for quite some time, but more significantly that particular Sat night truly epitomized how amazing and mutually expansive and full of sincere love and respect for one another our relationship is—cuddling in your bed & talking that particular night really embodied the most cherished aspects of our relationship because I absolutely love being affectionate with you, I love touching you, running my fingers through you hair, caressing your arms, holding your hand, kissing you; but I also absolutely love talking to you about the revolution, about music, art, your dreams and desires, philosophies, ways of being and thinking, and specifically that night about the development of your persona as a performer on stage and you as a revolutionary icon in everyday life. Then to top it off, we had sex, which I also absolutely love because I love being and feeling that incredibly close to you: becoming one with you and becoming multiple at the same time. I feel so comfortable and so much love for you and so intensely close to you when we make love, and I'm fairly sure you feel the same way—this mutual sharing of feelings for one another (and our mutual desire to continually expand) is what makes sex with you (and our relationship in general) so fucking amazing, expansive, and somewhat unique or at least rare... If you can't already tell, I've been extremely nostalgic (which we both agreed is an unexpansive exercise), reminiscing, going thru a week-to-week, day-to-day, hour-to-hour account of the development of our relationship from the very first words I spoke to you, thinking fondly of memories we've made together (I am also exceedingly aware that we've only known each other for 4-5 months and that we've only been RPL's for less than 2 of those months, so I am aware how silly this whole nostalgic exercise is that I've been indulging in, but I also know the intensity of feelings and thoughts we have shared; so for me it's about the levels [or quality, as people often say] rather than the time [or quantity]). But what the fuck, I'm sitting in jail waiting to go to prison so I'm giving myself a little leeway in terms of engaging in unexpansive exercises, especially if it's providing me with some happiness in this horribly life-sucking coffin they call a jail cell.

By the way, it's now Friday 8/22/08. I've been working on this letter, off and on, for three days now. I don't have your address so I just keep writing and writing and writing... I woke up this morning feeling more depressed than usual... I just spoke to you on the phone so I won't get into what I was gonna write 'cause I basically just told you on the phone. It's so nice to hear your voice! It's so warm and soothing, your voice that is—obviously. [. . .] I cannot wait to see you on Sunday! It's gonna be so nice to see your handsome face and to look into your eyes when we talk. I'm excited about seeing Monika and Laura tomorrow too. Wow, visits are great. It's amazing how much of a better mood I'm in now after talking to you and confirming your visit and learning 'bout Monika and Laura's visit—especially compared to this morning when I woke and I actually contemplated having dope smuggled into the jail and how I'm gonna make a binkie (i.e., old school syringe) so I could shoot it and waste the day away nodding off in my cell or possibly even o.d. But that was way early this morning and now I don't feel like that anymore. I actually started feeling better during drug education class; so don't worry, my moods are not wholly dependent on you—so no pressure, k. You're just my icing on the cake that I already have, which is me—I'm a cake :). So back to my drug education class, I again totally participated with great enthusiasm and fervor. The class focused on relationships. I emphasized establishing and developing a loving and expansive relationship with oneself first, which would then inform how one relates to others and the types of people one desires to form relationships. At the end, after listening to many of the girls describe abusive-type relationships (often coming from both partners in the relationship), I realized that these girls consciously or unconsciously glamorize this kind of abusive-/hardcore-like romantic relationships (many of them are lesbians too) just like I glamorized the hardcoreness of heroin addiction. I tried to explain this to the class, specifically to this one girl but she got defensive. She started getting angry but the other girls at her table who understood or at least respected what I was saying calmed her down. As a side note (which I think I already knew but hoped it wasn't so prevalent), most prisoners are highly religious, very into Jesus Christ and the Lord. It's unfortunate because the one girl who seems the most expansive, the most thoughtful and intelligent is also the most Jesus-obsessed. She thinks I'm scorned or removed or disillusioned (I forgot the exact words she used) because of my disdain for capitalism, which she views as an inherent social mode of existence. It's interesting, yet exceedingly sad, that these are the people who are suppose to be the rebels of society, the non-conformists, the rule-breakers—ones we might think would aid the revolution—yet due to the highly oppressive (and repressive) judicial system and prison/jail system, these people turn into religious freaks who desire nothing more than to conform to society's norms—damn, that's a powerful set of systems. On the other hand, most prisoners re-offend so what's that about?! Is it just talk while they're in here as a coping mechanism? Or maybe it takes a few times being locked up. Or maybe it's something deeper, something beyond one's control or understanding (much like alcoholism, perhaps). If it is something beyond their control, then we may as well guide them toward our cause—if they're gonna break laws anyway, they may as well be laws that [if broken] will lead to more expansion for everyone on this planet and beyond, right? What do you think?

[...] I'm running out of paper so I'm gonna finally end this super long and somewhat loquacious (although it's hard to be wordy handwriting—much easier to be gaudy typing) letter. I love you and miss you with all my heart and being. Hope you are happy, revolutionary, creative, and continually expanding...

Your RPL,
Jennifer Moon

. . .

CRDF (Century Regional Detention Facility), Lynwood, CA

Monday, 8/25/08

My Dearest, One and Only R.P.L.,

Thank you for talking to me on the phone for an extended amount of time yesterday—it somewhat made up for our missed visit or at least eased the pain greatly. I also want to apologize for talking so much 'cause I know you kind of dislike conversations where you feel you cannot get a word in edgewise. I know you say you don't mind but I at least want you to know that I am highly aware of my recent incessant talking and that I will try to cut it down so that our future phone conversations are more of a mutual exchange. I can also say for certain that my increased chattering is definitely due to nervousness, slight insecurities, and my current situation. It seems that I've been using situational reasons to explain or excuse many of my recent and more blatant unexpansive behaviors and thinking patterns. On the one hand, I can definitely understand how my extreme situation and environment can easily lend itself to feelings of loneliness, insecurity, anxiety, depression, etc. Yet, on the other hand, it's often through intense, extreme situations like this that one can more authentically see a person for who s/he truly is—it is the manner in which one handles oneself in trying situations that tends to be the most revealing about that person. I remember the first time you told me that you liked me [...] while giving me a hug you said how proud or impressed you were of how I was handling all my court shit: my case as well as my strained relationship with Colin—you said I was handling it with such grace and dignity. I want to walk through this with grace and dignity as well; and I apologize for putting unnecessary pressure on you to constantly tell me things to reassure me of your feelings for me and the status of our relationship (which is humorous 'cause I've always stressed the formlessness of our relationship), especially if you are just not capable of telling me what I want to hear (this is not to say you don't love me or that you don't properly express your love and commitment to me—it's more about my insecurities and trying to get you to feed into them). By the way, I'm severely hoping that this will be the last time I bring up all this shit regarding you, me, and our relationship. I know we discussed most of this over the phone and you may feel like I'm simply reiterating or beating a dead horse but if I find myself still thinking about an issue(s), then it's obviously not completely worked thru or resolved for me; and in addition, I always feel better once I write something out because then I can be as thorough and specific as I need to be in order to feel that I said everything I needed to say and that the other party (i.e., you) is clear on my stance and my feelings so there is little possibility for misinterpretation and miscommunication. You also know that this type of writing activity is an obsessive/compulsive indulgence of mine so... I guess keep that in mind—I'm not perfect as you well know and I'm human too as you've pointed out to me on a few occasions.

So, I want to first go back and discuss my current waffling between my situational insecurities and my desire to maintain my expansive nature/tendencies/outlook (or "walk" with dignity and grace). The manner and degree in which I jump back and forth, from one extreme to another, can not only be exhausting, time consuming, and anxiety ridden, but also confusing to the person (namely you) who I express ideas/speculations based on such seemingly opposing, dichotomous ends. And I'm specifically referring to what I expressed to you over the phone (as well as in my last letter): how in one sentence I say I want you to wait for me and in the very next sentence I'm telling you to go date someone (under certain stipulated conditions) if you need to in order to avoid severe loneliness—and these two ideas confused you because they seem to be mutually exclusive of one another or at least cancel each other out. But to me it seems so obviously transparent that when I tell myself (and you) that I expect you to date if you need/want to, it's a coping mechanism for me to avoid possible heartache—much in the same manner you tell yourself that you will eventually loose (in one way or another) everything/everyone you love. So of course I do not want you to date, get romantically involved/committed to another person while I'm locked up—it would sadden me to no end. But I cannot control nor predict the future (although I do think we can shape it to a large extent by maintaining integrity to our values and beliefs and desires) so I must be open to the possibility of you falling in love with someone other than me, especially since you claim to fall in love so easily. This morning I thought of another way my speculative statement may confuse you, which I didn't think of before because I was always thinking of it from my stance.

But when I thought how I would feel if you said a similar thing to me, I realized I may feel a bit hurt, wondering why you are seemingly pushing me to date in your absence—as if you didn't care if I stayed with you or not. I don't know if you felt this way or not; but if you did, I apologize. My intentions were quite the opposite—it was coming from a deep, sincere love and respect for you. I want to love you expansively, which means I try hard to not think of you in a possessive manner: I want you to be the happiest and the most expansive and feel the most love, even if it's not with me (but of course I'd prefer it if you choose to share your life intimately with me). Mariah Carey sings it best in one of her songs (which I can't remember the name, but which I'm sure you'll hate, yet it really is an expansivelove song): "If you love someone, let him go; and if he comes back to you, then you'll know it's true." Those may not be the exact lyrics but the concept is correct and highly expansive, don't you think?... But I think in my case, I'm being a bit martyrish. By suggesting that you date in my absence and if you do decide to date and then fall in love with another, I then get to be that martyr—I get to be right about the fact that love is always going to be a tragic romance for me, love will always allude me in some tragically romantic scenario. This exceedingly romantic yet highly tragic notion could definitely fuel me for some time, but I just decided that I don't want to manipulate martyrdom into my life anymore (especially just for the sake of martyrdom). So I'm just going to say what I really want and I don't care how unexpansive it may sound. I want you to wait for me. I don't want you to date anyone in my absence. I expect when I get out that we will simply pick up where we left off. And I expect that our love for one another and our relationship will continue to grow, expand, and deepen—as will our revolutionary endeavors. All I ask is that if you do not feel the same way, that you tell me; and if in the course of my absence, your feelings change, then please inform me asap. And this will most definitely be the absolute last time I bring up this shit because I'm sure you're thinking (as I am) that this is gonna be a fucking long ass 7-9 months if I keep rehashing this shit over and over again ('cause it's been exactly one week since I've been incarcerated and I've mentioned some concern or issue regarding our relationship or your feelings for me, what like every friken time we talked or in every letter I've written so far). I do sincerely apologize for putting pressure on you and for my insecurities, which I'm sure are not very attractive or at least not very graceful or dignified. The thing is, I know you love me dearly and I know you plan to wait for me and I know you desire a relationship with me as much as I do with you. I also trust in your love and respect for me that you will always tell me if things/feelings/situations have changed. I promise I will not doubt your love again, for when we were together I had no question—I could feel it. In fact, I emphasized and pushed the formlessness of our relationship (which I'm determined to return to because I do believe it to be expansive). I didn't need to nor did I necessarily desire you to tell me with your words how much you love me and are committed to this relationship—it would have been redundant and I much preferred your feelings for me revealed through interactions, sharing, and activities. [...] I just received two more of your letters and many of the words you wrote truly warmed my heart and I felt closer to you and truly loved by you—thank you. I love you... And I also want to tell you that my intense feelings of love for you is not situational—the urgency I feel and my obsessive/compulsive indulgences regarding my seeming need to tell you at every chance I get how I feel about you and our relationship is most definitely situational though. My feelings for you have not changed nor grown exponentially since being incarcerated—I have always felt this intensely about you, us, and the revolution. The only thing that has changed are the structural elements: the manners in which I express my feelings and love for you...

[...] (Wednesday, 8/27/08) I just got off the phone with you—just hearing your voice can fill me with joy for the entire day (and sometimes for more than a day). And as I mentioned to you on the phone, I also received your fourth letter written Friday, 8/22/08. After reading this letter, all my insecurities regarding your feelings for me disappeared all together. Not that I want you to feel pain regarding our separation nor do I want you to loose faith in yourself and your incredible talents: hearing this saddens and upsets me to the point where I also get angry at myself for committing such a violent, selfish, and senseless act against another human being, which caused our separation and me not being there for you during a crucial point in your life. This is in no way an excuse, but I truly feel that the only reason I committed such a horrible crime against another person was wholly due to drugs: the intense degree of sheer terror and desperation that I felt at the prospect of being dope sick and not having a "wake-up" after 4 ½ years of shooting dope every fuckin' day was too much for me to think in terms of acceptance and letting go and of others. I can honestly say with near certainty that I would never even think of committing such crimes against humanity (no matter how seemingly abominable an individual or group may be) clean and sober. And if you recall, I couldn't even follow through on the violent aspect of the crime: I may not have had a problem punching the numbers on the keypad or even getting the victim's attention, but I couldn't bring myself to pepper-spray him. Although I know that that doesn't matter 'cause I had no problem letting it happen and being a part of it and planning it. I know I really need to think about all this and truly understand and accept how horrible it was and to feel sincere remorse for the victim. I am still working on this; but I can at least say that I do not desire in any way, even in the remotest minute way, to engage in any violent act against humanity/the world/the universe, and this includes within the revolution as well—and for this I credit you.

[...] It's interesting how you can both make my stay here tolerable and unbearable at the same time—simultaneously encompassing both ends of a spectrum (therefore breaking out of dichotomies). On one hand, the temporary loss of you and our forced separation is the primary reason why it is so incredibly difficult for me to be here. Temporary removal from "normal" life and even from my dearest friends would perhaps not be so bad (especially for only 9 months)—it's my ties to you specifically, which makes incarceration unbearable at times. Yet at the same time, it is because of you, your love for me, your support, your commitment to me, your desire and plan to wait for me that I am able to tolerate being here and even at times enjoy myself and laugh and have a pleasant and positive attitude and outlook. Because as you had said in your letter, without you everything could go to shit and I wouldn't care. If I didn't have you by my side, if I didn't have you to come home to, I could easily see myself falling into a deep depression and saying fuck it and use and possibly assimilate into prison life. I am so grateful that I have you even though it tears me apart to be away from you for such an extended amount of time.

What I do want you to be assured of is that I am just fine in here. For the first five or so days, I was admittedly severely depressed—to have you and my amazingly developing life taken away so abruptly was a bit too much for me to handle initially. But I am adapting and as you so elegantly mentioned in one of your letters, I am finding the beauty in the small, simple things around me and thru my interactions with others. I am making friends and find myself laughing a lot and bringing laughter and joy to others. I think it also helped tremendously that I got moved out to the dayroom, so now I'm no longer locked in a 4' x 12' cell all day and night with the exception of optional programming based on the moods of whatever deputy is currently on duty. I will tell you more details regarding my day-to-day life in jail when I speak to you on the phone so that I have something other than repeating what I write in my letters to talk to you about. I also want to respond to each of your letters but I want to get this letter out to you tonight. I'll start another one tomorrow.

I love you. Please don't loose faith in yourself because you are simply the most amazing, inspirational, passionate, and talented person I know. I miss you so tremendously it truly aches.

Love with Intensity and Fervor,
Jennifer Moon
(your beloved RPL)

• • •

CRDF (Century Regional Detention Facility), Lynwood, CA

Friday, 9/12/08

My Dearest, Most Cherished and Loved Jonathan — ♥ ♥ ♥ ♥

I was woken up this morning around 5 am by the deputy delivering yesterday's mail. What a lovely way to be woken and to start the day with your beautiful letter(s) and the wonderful feeling of being loved by you. I miss you so very much. It helps, though, to have pictures of you. Thank you so much for sending them. As I mentioned to you on the phone, I taped all of them right above my head, less than a foot away from my face. And every night, I kiss each one of your photos, tell you goodnight and I love you, and wish you sweet and/or expansive/transcendent dreams. Then every morning I get to wake up to your handsome face with your beautiful blue eyes looking back at me; and on some mornings, when I still have not completely awoken from my dreamy state, for just a split second, I imagine that you are really here with me—that what I'm looking at is not an image at all but actually you in the flesh—and then that wonderfully transcendent moment and feeling quickly fades back into reality. I imagine it to be similar to that one morning you experienced when you awoke thinking about me outside the defining and limiting boundaries of our separation. I too am extremely grateful for moments like these—even if it's only for a split second. And to complete my disclosure of my evening and morning rituals, every morning when I wake, I again give you kisses, tell you good morning, I love you, and wish you a lovely, beautiful, and expansive/transcendent day. So I too hope that you are able to feel the kisses, hugs, love, and affection I feel and project to you every morning, evening, and throughout the day. I love you, my darling ♥...

As a side note, I do like the word, "transcendent," as an alternative and/or additive to the overly-used word, "expansive." I remember at the time (during grad school), when I was trying to pick a word that would most accurately describe the concepts/ideals embodied currently within "expansive" and "unexpansive," I did think of words similar to "transcendent" (I don't recall if I debated that particular word though). The reason I decided against words like "transcendent" is because it implied to me, especially during that time, ideas and feelings of being better than others—that I'm somehow existing on a higher plane than everyone else. On some level, existing in a constant state of hyper-awareness and continuous expansion (or constant state of becoming, as perhaps D&G would describe it) is indeed existing on an alternate plane than most everyone on this planet. And perhaps, also, I am bringing ideas and feelings like 'better than' and 'higher' to words like "transcendent" because of my own personal inability to detach from thinking [*within*] dichotomies (i.e., existing on an alternate plane does not need to translate to better or higher). Yet, in addition, I don't know if you're aware of this or not, but I am extremely hyper-sensitive and careful to not portray myself as believing that I am better than others or worse, pretentious. This is why I sometimes go to the opposite degree and emphasize my naïveté, my dreamy idealism, and sci-fi-based fantasies. In order for us to succeed as adored revolutionary icons, we both must be easily accessible to the public. We must be able to blend within the public as well as intensely stand-out from it, simultaneously—therefore breaking out of dichotomous modes of being and entering a revolutionary, expansive, transcendent way of being. And once again, I think it begins with achieving a delicate balance between two extremes: knowing the correct time and place to access whatever end of the spectrum, being able to switch back and forth at will and immediately, possibly demanding more and more at a quicker rate, until one day we may surprisingly find ourselves truly occupying both ends of the spectrum at precisely the same exact moment. This describes one process of breaking free from dichotomous modes of being. The other is to just exist only on one side of the spectrum—the expansive side, such as love (as opposed to hate) or niceness (as opposed to meanness)—until the unexpansive end of the spectrum simply ceases to exist and a wholly new way of being comes into play that our current imagination (which is bound by ingrained and unconscious dichotomies) cannot even fathom as of yet. I know I just went off on a tangent. So to bring it back to the word, "transcendent," after all that I said regarding its possible connotations, do you still prefer this word over "expansive"? I know that I can be overly critical and concerned about certain things, so please tell me what you think. I do agree with you, way back when, when you suggested we build a glossary of terms to describe and be utilized in the revolution. I don't know if "transcendent" was intended for that (actually I know that you were suggesting it as an alternative to "expansive") but it made me think of the glossary of revolutionary terms anyways.

I agree with you that when I get out we should just engage in continuous sex for about a month, to get it all out of our systems so to speak—indulge in various sex-capades. I would love a strap-on for a home-cuming present, for both of us :). [...] I hope this doesn't make you feel unusual, in a bad way. Because it definitely is a sexual deviance from the norm, for both of us. Yet again, this ability and desire for both of us to switch sexual roles of dominance and submission, to penetrate and be penetrated—usually delineated to male and female respectively—is another example of how we break out of dichotomies. We are so friken expansive and transcendent, even down to the base level of erotic desires and biological passions. We are so perfectly suited for one another, it's a bit unreal or uncanny at times. I love you, honey... and I can't wait to fuck you with a strap-on. By the way, do you enjoy other forms of dominance, which involve more role-playing, such as dominatrix-type play? I've never done it; but if you're into it, I can certainly learn.

It's interesting that you love the part in anti-oedipus when they reference D.H. Lawrence talking about psychoanalysis in terms of sexuality (i.e., casting sexuality as a kind of "dirty little secret"), but then you continue perpetuating the idea of sexuality being a "dirty little secret" by being overly-concerned that someone may read about your sexual desires—as if you are ashamed or embarrassed of your desires. It's amazing to me that you can be so incredibly expansive and transcendent when it comes to sexual practices and desires; yet you become incredibly repressed at the notion of such desires and practices being made known to the public. In fact, most of your issues and concerns revolve around what other people think of you, wouldn't you agree? This unnecessary yet often overpowering concern, preoccupation, and stress regarding the thoughts and feelings of others in relation to oneself is the primary reason why I began pushing the idea of breaking down the division between public and private space. Because it's not only about breaking down private, material ownership but also breaking down the family unit and destroying secrets and the power of ownership secrets can have over people. And I'm speaking mainly of secrets that have the potential to cause shame and/or embarrassment...

Ok, before I continue with this subject, I need to let out some steam. I just got in an argument with Mac 10: well it was more like me going off on her on some diatribe in which she had no response, either because she didn't understand me or she knew she wouldn't be able to argue against me. In either case, this is a perfect example of how one perpetuates one's own repression and, worse, the repression of others (because it wouldn't be so detrimental if the result was the repression of the one individual who's perpetuating said repression; but the unfortunate result is that it represses all). And this may give some clue or insight on the terribly important question posed in anti-oedipus of "Why does one desire one's own repression?" And the sad fact is that in most cases people are not even aware that what they are doing ultimately results in the unknowing desire and perpetuation of everyone's repression, including their own. In Mac's case, her self-desiring and self-perpetuating repression came in the form of kissing the ass of authority and wanting to be "right." It's funny, yet sad, how some of these institutionalized, gang-banging fuckers talk all tough and hard; but when it comes down to it, they're nothing but authority ass-kissers and finger-pointers (tattle-tales, snitches). Mac is an extreme case though because even though she's been to prison many times, I don't believe she's a gang-banger at heart—she's way too sweet and friendly, especially compared to other self-proclaimed gang-bangers here. Plus her aunt's a sheriff so that helps inform her behavior towards authority figures as well. Before I tell you what happened this morning (Sunday, 9/14/08), I'm gonna have to tell you about the build-up first because if I don't, you're gonna think I'm over-reacting. Ok, for the past couple of days I've been getting exceedingly annoyed with Mac because if someone's talking loud in their cell, Mac'll yell out, "Cell 13's being loud!" or if someone's sitting in front of the TV when she's maybe not suppose to, Mac will yell out, "Bunk 54 Up is watching TV!" In the beginning it was kind of funny 'cause Mac was doing it mostly to her friends as a kind of joke (jokin' on the square perhaps). For example, Mac and this stud-broad, Dre (who, by the way, looks exactly like a dude: if you saw her on the streets you would just assume she was a guy), have this kind of love/hate relationship. In the evenings, Dre would sometimes yell out her cell to her girlfriend who's out in the dayroom. The deputy would scream, "Who's yellin' like that?!" And Mac would reply, "That's Hamilton, cell 12, Low!" And we would all laugh, including Dre. But last night, Mac's little tattle-taling was getting out of control and she also started stirring up racial issues with it. So last night, Deputy Chavez was on duty and she can be a bit more lax than other deputies. So some girls out in the dayroom were wandering around and watching TV. Chavez also popped open cell 5 for some reason, so those two girls were out wandering as well. It may be true that Deputy Chavez may play favorites or it may be that she's just incredibly lax and all one needs to do is ask. But in either case, who really fucking cares. The way I see it, if you're out wandering, socializing, and/or watching TV during non-program time and you can get away with it, then good for you. But then again, I'm not one to get jealous or feel that it's unfair or feel personally slighted in some way. I mean, it may be unfair, but there are so many more intensely unfair and oppressive things to be concerned about. So Mac was getting all upset about this and getting all the girls in the next bunk over all upset too. You know how I hate describing people in terms of race/ethnicity but it's necessary in this case because Mac made it racial. So all the girls who are in the bunk next to ours happen to be black and all the girls wandering/watching TV happen to be Latina. And the funny thing is that Mac happens to be half black and half Mexican. Obviously Mac was channeling her African-American side because she kept stirring shit up by saying stuff like, "You know why they're all out there—look at the color of their skin," and "Ms. Chavez plays favorites—all those girls are from her hood" (figuratively), and "You know if we went out there, we'd all get in trouble 'cause we're black!" Mac was talking so much shit that one of the poor girls in the bunk next to ours, Cynthia (who seems to me to be a terrible follower and easily influenced), started getting off her bunk to walk over to the girls watching TV and try to start shit with them. In the end, it all culminated with Mac obnoxiously yelling, "Deputy, is it program time? I'm just wondering if it's program time?" Mac yelled this a few times and even B (Beatrice who's definitely the most expansive of the black girls involved in these shenanigans) kept telling her to shut-up and saying, "Why you gotta say shit like that?" and "Why you trying to do the deputy's job?" And all this time, I'm lying in my bunk under Mac, reading my book and listening to all this shit. I wanted to say something a couple times but I was way too tired to get involved. But to give Mac some credit, after it all died down a bit, I think Mac became aware of her making it a racial issue and jokingly yelled down to me, "Now I'm really gonna make it racial. Hey Korea [which she never calls me that], did I just hear you call me nigger!?" I laughed because it was funny in its unexpected awareness. So that's all the background, which led up to my outburst this morning. My god that took longer than I thought; and now I'm kind of over it, but I spent so much time setting it up, I feel obligated to finish it. I only hope all this is somewhat interesting to you and not just the reactionary ramblings of an angry person. Anyways, so this morning during breakfast I got super annoyed because the deputy wouldn't let us get hot water (for coffee, and she usually does but she said no because another deputy was there). I was complaining about it (because coffee is my one joy in this dismal existence) and Mac said, "I don't know what you're complaining about. Hot water is a privilege. Miss C is being nice when she gives it to us." My response was "Fuck that! Hot water is a right, not a privilege," which I said half jokingly. Then Snow continued on by explaining that other modules have their hot water pot out so that people can just get some whenever or they have a hot water spout by the sink. So I said to Mac, "See so they're using hot water here as a form of control and power." And as Snow and I were leaving the table, I overheard Mac telling B, "These bitches act like they know shit, talking like they know what's going on..." I think she was referring mostly to Snow but in any case, it made me mad, not only because she was talking shit about me and my friend but also because Mac often does the same thing (ex., the fact that she thought she knew what was going on the night before with the Latinas and Deputy Chavez). So it got worse and all came to a head when Mac came back to our bunk and as she was climbing up to her bed told me, "Miss C's gonna make an announcement to let you know that hot water is a privilege." I was like, "What?! You went up there and fuckin' told her I was complaining about it?!" Mac responded, "Yeah, but it's not just you. It's to let everyone know." I was so fuckin' pissed at this time, I couldn't help but go on a little rant about the constructs of power and control and how she's feeding into it and how she's just kissing ass and wanting to be "right" yet her need to prove she's "right" just perpetuates her own repression because ideas like privilege, especially in relation to things like hot water, is a concept developed by authoritative power to control us and why would she want to perpetuate this power-driven concept of privilege by reminding the police of it, basically saying they're "right" and please repress us more... Come to think of it, I think Mac is bright enough to have understood me (or at least, get the general idea); and hopefully she didn't respond because she knew I was correct on some level. But it made me realize more that most people don't know what the fuck they're doing and they are totally unaware of how their thoughts, behaviors, actions perpetuate their own desire for their own repression. So I'm becoming more and more convinced that the majority of the population will have to be "tricked" or persuaded, using the various tools offered by popular culture (including religious-type sermons), to join the revolution. Ok, now that I finally finished my stupid story, I can return to my previous topic.

As I was saying, feelings of shame and embarrassment are the emotions that generally cause me the most grief and also the ones that seem to linger on for eternity. Therefore, as a way for me to minimize or eliminate these uncomfortable emotions, I decided to always expose myself completely—reveal all my "secrets," never create new ones, and be painfully open about everything. I know at times I can go over the top with this, and there are also things that I still struggle to openly reveal, especially things which happened during my childhood; but for the most part, I'm fairly rigorous with this practice. Because if I make public personal shit about me that society may deem as shameful and/or embarrassing and if I publicly own it, talk about it openly with confidence or at least without shame, then it can never be used against me to cause me pain in the form of intense and often paralyzing shame and/or embarrassment (even though I may still feel somewhat shameful or embarrassed about it). Now all of this led up to the overarching idea of breaking down the boundaries that delineate public and private space, which includes the family unit, sex and sexuality, and other issues deemed personal or private. Do you feel shameful or embarrassed about your sexual desires? Is that why you are concerned about someone potentially reading about it or finding out about it? Or is there some other issue I'm totally missing? I know you don't completely agree with full and complete disclosure of all personal issues. I must also remind myself that I was about your age when I completely gave into this idea. So maybe you'll eventually change your mind and slowly realize the complete and absolute freedom it can give you. I hope I don't sound too condescending. I just want you to be comfortable with your sexuality and also not care so much what other people think of you (not only in regards to your sexual desires). I just got off the phone with you. In our conversation, I brought up this issue and you agreed with me that I was being a bit condescending. I really don't mean to be. I just think that not feeling comfortable to behave or be yourself at a party or controlling your facial expressions as a way to control how other people read you seems stressful, confining, and exhausting. And after talking to you, I understand that it has less to do with feelings of shame and embarrassment and more to do with fear of punishment or unpleasant consequences. And I apologize for dumping on you on the phone (and in this letter) regarding stupid, petty arguments I have with my fellow prisoners. It seemed to have maybe bummed you out or at least negatively affected our phone conversation. And I apologize if this letter affects you in a similar manner. I love you; and thank you for always being there for me, even for unexpansive moments when I need to vent :).

[…] You know what my favorite part of your letter(s) is? When you wrote how you told Maggie that you "could live in a painted and converted bus with [me] in the parking lot on Venice Beach when we're old." I too could be very happy living with you on a bus. Or even as nomads wandering the earth with no home and no possessions—as long as I'm with you. And I also think about growing old with you. I look forward to the many days and nights and years we will share together and all the multitude of amazing adventures we can reminisce about when we're old, living in a painted, converted bus :).

I LOVE YOU,
Jennifer (your R.P.L.)

• • •

CRDF (Century Regional Detention Facility), Lynwood, CA

Thursday, 9/18/08

Dearest Jonathan — ♥

My dear, dear, sweet Jonathan who is no longer available by phone between the hours of 9:30 am to preferably 6:30 pm Monday thru Friday. I tried calling you today twice around 4 and 4:30 pm. But alas, you are a man of your word and did not pick up as you had informed me you would no longer be able to do. And oh what a sad, sad tragedy it is that we so rarely program in the early mornings or evenings, especially during the week. So it seems, my darling, our phone relationship has begun to diminish perhaps toward non-existent, which may not be too horrible a loss since we both despise the phone. I'm sorry I'm behaving/writing so strangely. Actually what I would like to do is rip all the phones off the columns upon which they are hung and hurl them across the room at the deputy for no good reason except pure confused frustration, which can easily turn into aggression. I want so desperately to talk to you and that is making me upset as well. […]

Ok, it's now the next day, Friday, 9/19/08. Hey, I have six months continuous sobriety today! The longest I've ever had. Too bad I can't go around town to a bunch of meetings and collect my 6 month chips ('cause I've never taken a clean one before). In any case, it's a brand new day. It's around 7:30 am, I just ate breakfast; and I'm now drinking a cup of coffee and writing my most favorite person in the world, who I also happen to be madly in love with. What could be better?! Actually you and I both know tons of things better than my current incarceration. I'm just trying to think positive because I woke up still in somewhat of a foul mood. Although last night I did release some tension singing a collage of songs (from Joni Mitchell, Whitney Houston, and Wilson Phillips to Bright Eyes, BabyShambles, and BRMC) for the listening pleasure of my fellow prisoners—whether they liked it or not. Jonathan, I'm really beginning to hate it here and I think I'm starting to get resentful. I even started to get mad at you last night for not answering my desperate calls. Of course I know—and I sincerely hope you also know—that my minimal, abrupt, and fleeting resentment toward you last night was completely unreasonable and horribly displaced. Let me just tell you what's been bothering me these past few days.

So to begin, I've been here for exactly one month as of yesterday. And although I don't mind terribly that I'm still here because I get to see you every weekend, I started getting concerned that the reason I'm still in Lynwood is because either the defense or the prosecution is planning to subpoena me for Colin's case (his next court date is 10/08). And I know you're not gonna be too thrilled about this but Colin has been writing me a significant amount (five letters so far) and he still really really wants me to write a letter for him for court. On a separate note, I've written Colin twice—but I have yet to tell him about us. I feel I need to ease into that one; although he will most likely be able to guess by the distant, non-intimate tone and language of my letters. […]

[…] I love you, Jonathan. I need to end this letter now so I can add it to tonight's mail (Monday, 9/22/08). As of this morning, I was still SP0. We spoke a lot on the phone over the weekend and during your visit so I think I responded to everything in your three letters (including your hot sex letter, which reminds me that I'm gonna work on another sex letter for you next), and I also discussed the issues which were causing me grief during the middle of last week. So unless my SP status changes tonight, it seems I will be here until at least Thursday, which means I'll get commissary tomorrow, which means I can call you Wednesday (and hopefully we'll program during a time you can talk). It was nice to talk to you even for a couple minutes this morning. And I meant what I said regarding being over worrying about you and our relationship. Deep in my heart I trust the love that we share and I trust that we are true R.P.L.'s. You had once wrote in one of your earlier letters that I should delve into my heart, not my mind, for comfort and answers regarding your love for me and the status of our relationship—and that is what I'm doing...

With complete trust in love: our love,
Your R.P.L.,
Jennifer ☾

• • •

CRDF (Century Regional Detention Facility), Lynwood, CA

Wednesday, 9/24/08

My Dearest Jonathan — ♥

The majority of my down time (i.e., the times we are confined to our bunks) these past few days have been spent fantasizing about you. On numerous occasions I've tried to delve into three different novels, each time my mind uncontrollably wanders to thoughts of you. And not just any of the number of charming and adoring thoughts/scenarios/memories I have of you, but rather highly erotic and detailed scenarios of you fucking me... from behind, for example, holding my hips firmly in place with both hands so you can force your hard cock into my tight, wet pussy. My slender body falls forward, accentuating my hourglass figure: my small waist and my perfectly rounded ass lifted high in the air, begging to be fucked. Your grasp around my hips tightens as you aggressively pull me back onto your stiff cock, over and over again, each time thrusting your throbbing dick deeper and harder into me. I scream out with increasing pleasure. Oh my god, Jonathan, I want to scream now just to release my intense yearning for you. My pussy is so wet right now. I would give anything to feel you inside of me. For you to fuck me over and over again and when you are about to cum, pull your swelling prick out dripping wet with my sweet juices and force it into my mouth so I can suck you off until you cum deep into my mouth. Oh I'm so sorry Jonathan, I got ahead of myself again. I was planning on writing you an actual erotic story, much like yours, with an actual beginning or establishing scene to build arousal. But once again, I was incredibly too horny for foreplay. Shit, I hope I'm not this horrible a lover in real life. I just returned from masturbating in the bathroom. And as you had wrote regarding looking at porn, my fingers inside my pussy is a poor substitute for your beautiful penis and your strong, muscular hands and the way only you can touch me. We're about to program, so when I return maybe I'll give it another shot and write you an erotic story deserving of you.

[…] You know I have this fantasy of you fucking me in public. That time we had sex in the backyard at Felicity, I got turned on by the idea that someone may be watching us and the potential of being caught. This is not to say that I would want to actually get caught because that might be slightly embarrassing—it's the idea that we could get caught, which gives it a heightened sense of arousal due to a feeling of desperation and extreme naughtiness with potential for "danger." I also get turned on by the idea that someone is secretly getting aroused watching us fuck. I don't know if you feel the same way because the idea of getting in trouble or potentially dangerous situations is a source of fear for you rather than arousal. And if you get embarrassed getting a boner in public, then engaging in actual sex in public must be unthinkable. Although it may be different because you have a partner to join in your wanton desires and erotic transgressions, which could persuade you to loose yourself in uncontrollable passion and forget all your fears. Plus you look fucking hot when you screw me so you shouldn't be embarrassed if someone is watching. But whatever, hopefully you'll enjoy this anyways...

It is a warm, summer evening, the sun has just set and we are standing in a long, crowded line for some highly publicized event. I am wearing a short skirt, tight enough to show the outline of my ass and a form-fitting t-shirt accentuating my figure and the fullness of my breasts. I have heels on, which gives me the added height to place my ass almost even with your groin. I am standing in front of you with my back facing you and our attention is on a young, attractive couple openly making out in public. The young man's arousal increases as we watch his hands caress her full breasts and grab her ass pulling her pelvis against his. Your attention returns to me as you notice my nipples hardening underneath my tight t-shirt. You place your right hand on my soft belly as I push my ass up against your swelling cock. I reach behind me and begin rubbing your thigh and groin, lightly brushing your now stiff rod with my hand. I notice everyone's attention is on the young couple aggressively making out, so I grab your left hand and force it underneath my short skirt, in between my legs from behind. You feel the damp crotch of my panties and you can no longer resist. Pulling my wet panties to one side you slide your fingers in between my labia and begin caressing my clit. I flinch from the immediate and intense sensation. You continue rubbing my clit as you slide your finger inside my tight, soft pussy. I groan slightly. Suddenly you stick your thumb in my cunt for lubrication and shove it up my ass. I almost cry out but you stick your right hand fingers in my mouth to shut me up. With your thumb in my ass, you force your middle finger back up my cunt and rub my clit with your forefinger. My body quivers with heightened pleasure and I arch my back slightly to sink your fingers deeper into me. I am completely taken over by you, filling me up in every orifice. I desperately suck on your fingers as you begin aggressively fucking my pussy and ass with your other fingers. I can no longer hold back and start pounding my ass against your groin, fucking your fingers harder and faster. I am lost in intense pleasure, but you notice we are becoming conspicuous so you suddenly pull out of me and yank me out of line to an abandoned concession stand hidden in a darkened corner. You bend me over the counter, rip my panties down just above my knees and take a moment to admire my drenched pussy and round ass peaking out underneath my skirt. Then you quickly unzip your pants, pull your throbbing dick out and shove it deep into my cunt. I cry out as you groan with relieved pleasure. My warm, wet flesh feels so good around your stiff dick, tightly enveloping it completely. You grab my hips and slide your hard cock in and out of me. My pussy begins to contract and the sensation forces you to fuck me harder. You pound me over and over again against the counter, my tits smashed up against the glass and my hard nipples rubbing against the surface with every thrust. "Oh baby you feel so fucking good," I gasp as you continue to penetrate me, your pulsating prick sinking itself inside my cunt with more and more force, the sound of your pelvis rhythmically pounding against my ass. "You fuck me so good!" I scream. "I'm gonna cum," your voice straining as you pull your cock out dripping with my sweet juices, jacking yourself off until you shoot your cum all over my exposed ass and swollen, glistening pussy.

[…] Fuck I can just scream thinking about it! I think I better go masturbate before I explode. I'll be back...

Ok, I'm back but I didn't get to cum because a line was starting to form for the bathroom and it was making me nervous and self-conscious. Now this is an example where public sexual activity is definitely not a turn on. The potential for getting caught masturbating on a cell toilet in Lynwood County Jail is so not arousing. […] I need to end this letter now 'cause I'm gonna sweep for one of the trustees and then they're gonna pick up all the outgoing mail. I'll see you this weekend. I miss you dearly.

I Love You,
Jennifer ☾, R.P.L.

• • •

CRDF (Century Regional Detention Facility), Lynwood, CA

Sunday, 9/28/08

My Dearest Love — ♥

It was so wonderful to see you today, and it was great that our last visit was extra long too (and hopefully it'll be the last visit you'll ever have to make to Lynwood County Jail or at least the last one ever to visit me). You have been so good to me. You really do love me. I hope you know that I truly love you as well. [...]

I also want to comment how it made my heart warm when I read, "It was a beautiful night," regarding your experience with love the evening at the Venice Beach group. Now this is gonna sound really Pollyanna, but I really do think that love is the most wonderful and spectacular thing and feeling ever. And I'm not just talking about the love I feel and share for and with you, which is incredible and cherished on its own, separate realm. I'm also referring to the love I feel for life, the world, the universe and beyond, and every single person, animal, living thing in it. When I sit and really feel the love I feel for all existence, it is truly an indescribably amazing experience: it is during these times I feel the most expanded beyond myself. I no longer fear love because I don't expect anything in return for my genuine love I feel for the world and beyond. At this point in my life, I can't help but love everyone. And regarding you, I don't fear loving you as completely and as intensely as I do because, even though I have hopes and dreams and goals regarding our love and relationship, I am open to the possibility of you falling out of love with me and vice versa. I have experienced enough heartache and failed dreams of love to know that that is more than possible; but I have also experienced walking through seemingly unbearable and unrecoverable love-losts to know I will always love again and usually more intensely and more genuinely than the time before. So knowing these two things, I am able to completely give myself to you now, to love you with every substance of my being, the best way I know how in every present moment that we share together from now until we are hopefully old, gray, and wrinkled living in a bus on Venice Beach. And even if we break up tomorrow, it will not stop me from fully loving you today because, as you often like to point out, now is what matters the most. I hope this is all not too sappy (or gaudy) for you. It's just that I strive to be the most expansive and give the most I can at every given moment without fear of failure—and that includes loving you.

[…] I don't ever want to take you for granted. I want to continually delight you, surprise you, inspire you, excite you, and make you feel love and lustful arousal as if for the first time. I want us to be perpetually in a courtship stage yet also have the trust, openness, intimacy, bond, and foundation of a long-term relationship simultaneously—once again, existing on both sides of the spectrum simultaneously and therefore breaking out of or transcending dichotomies.

And it's because of this desire for me to continually stimulate you that I am concerned that our last visit together may not have been entirely satisfying for you. I left feeling that I didn't provide my share of intellectually stimulating conversation. And yet again, I believe a lot of it has to do with my current situation. Not only is it difficult to engage in expansive talk with two slates of bullet-proof glass between us, but I was also feeling sad and a little nervous about leaving for prison. […]

[…] I love you. I hope all my raunchy horniness doesn't burn you out or eventually turn you off. Unfortunately, I need to end this letter now so I can get it out tonight. […] I love you, Jonathan. Wish me luck in prison. I will miss hearing your sexy voice on the phone and seeing your handsome face every week. Until our next rendezvous...

Your Loving and Devoted R.P.L.,
Jennifer ☾

• • •

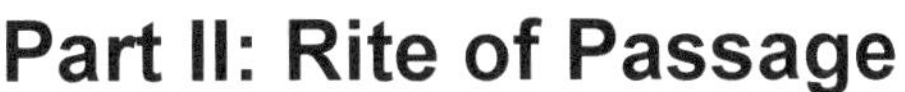

Part II: Rite of Passage

"Why do you lock yourself up in these chains?"
– Wilson Phillips

Wednesday, 10/01/08

Dearest Jonathan — ♥

My dear, darling, sweet, sexy, gorgeous love who is now so far away from me. As the address on the envelope indicates, I'm writing from central California as an official prisoner of Chowchilla. I even have a fancy CDC (California Department of Corrections) picture ID (I'm hoping I get to keep it when I leave). My CDC# or X# [...] is X33169. It's easy to remember because, besides the #1, they're all multiples of 3. And the last two digits are '69,' which given my recent obsession and preoccupation with sex (i.e., sex with you specifically and our mutual fascination with the 69 position) it seems highly appropriate. I even chuckled to myself, like an adolescent boy, when I found out my number.

So everything is fine now, today. But oh my fuckin' god, yesterday was a complete nightmare. And let me just preface what I'm about to describe by saying none of yesterday would have been nearly as bad (or maybe not even bad at all) if I didn't have a splitting headache the entire time due to the absence of coffee from my morning ritual (I also couldn't perform my daily morning bowel movement because we were woken up around 2 am to sit in a holding tank 'til around 6 am, was on the bus 'til around noon, and then sat in more holding tanks until around 6 pm; and we were told we could not "take a dump" in the bus toilet 'cause it's like an outhouse and would stink up the bus—not that I wanted to anyways 'cause we're chained to another prisoner—and I have trouble shitting in the holding tanks where the toilet's out in the open in a small crowded room full of women). But back to my horrible, paralyzing lack-of-coffee headache. I realized or, rather, was reminded ('cause I already knew this about myself) that I am a horrible sick person: I just cannot take or cope with pain very well. I guess that's why I was a heroin addict for so long. It's amazing to me what a different person I am when I'm sick or in prolonged pain. I suppose it's this way with most people. Maybe I just have a low tolerance for pain. And maybe it's also because I'm so exceedingly gregarious, charismatic, and witty normally :) that when I'm not feeling good to the point where I can't even talk or sit upright and my face drops in unattractive ways, the difference seems even more exaggerated. Monika will tell you that the difference from when I first came into Friendly House and just two or maybe three weeks after is like night and day. So basically, the way I was feeling yesterday, my first day at Chowchilla, is nothing like I feel now, which is perfectly fine, content, and somewhat excited/stimulated and definitely hyper-aware due to the brand new experience and environment.

[…] So on the bus ride up here, I kind of experienced a brief moment of happiness. The bus ride wasn't nearly as bad as I thought it would be nor nearly as long. I found it exceedingly pleasant to be able to watch the changing landscapes thru the windows (especially since I haven't seen the sky or the outdoors in six weeks). There was even one very brief moment, lasting maybe a second or two at the most, where I convinced myself that I was traveling thru some foreign land, like Europe. I don't know if you've ever experienced these surreal moments where you suddenly feel like you've been teleported to a foreign land and assume the perspective of a tourist or traveler. I love those moments; and I cherish and relish in them whenever I'm fortunate to experience them (I feel similarly for moments when I feel like I'm in a movie—it probably has to do with the fantastical element, which you know I love). So there was something about being woken up at 2 am and traveling slightly delirious from lack of sleep that reminded me of times Andy and I would travel in the middle of the night by Euro rail from country to country (as a way to maximize time and avoid unnecessary lodging costs) and awaken early in the morning in a new country: stepping out of the train station into a city I've never before seen in a sleepy daze was always so fantastical and dream-like—I loved it. I was also reminded of the times I traveled thru parts of Europe and Asia with my parents on tour buses. So by accessing a combination of those two memories, I was able to just momentarily transport myself outside of my current situation to that of a traveler or tourist of unknown, foreign lands (and in a sense I was indeed going to an unknown, foreign land). Even though this magical feeling lasted only a second or two, it was enough to make me smile and inform and alter my mood and attitude so that I didn't mind so much that I was on a CDC bus being transported to a prison four to six hours away from LA (and you) and shackled to the girl sitting next to me. My senses are always heightened and I am always intrigued and stimulated with brand new experiences, especially ones that promise adventure and the possibility of danger; and going to prison for the first time fits that criteria, so I may as well think of it as an adventure rather than punishment.

Coming to prison, however, has made me realize that I'm still fucked up in the head about all this. Now what I'm about to say is truly how I'm feeling at the moment (which means it could definitely change once I "go over the wall," meaning leave receiving and enter actual prison), but I am also highly aware that my thinking is in many ways unexpansive and definitely conforming to socially constructed ideas of hardcore coolness. Please don't hold it against me 'cause in other ways it's also a coping mechanism. So yesterday morning (Wednesday, my first morning in prison), I was sitting with some of the other new girls in our muumuus (for the first day and a half, before we get our oranges, we have to wear actual blue-with-white-polka-dotted muumuus: you know those shapeless dresses older, overweight women often wear) and I couldn't stop myself from thinking and feeling like I've graduated to some higher level, which I have of course. I have definitely graduated to a higher, more serious level of imprisonment, but I'm talking as if this is a desirable thing: like a rite of passage. I know many young gang-banging boys consider going to prison a rite of passage into manhood: they actually strive and desire to go to prison, whether overtly or subconsciously. And I use to scoff at those stupid gangster boys I'd meet in rehabs. Yet I'd be also intrigued and somewhat attracted to those guys who've already been to prison. You know I have issues with glamorizing/romanticizing things/behaviors/actions society has deemed "bad," like shooting heroin, committing certain crimes, ex-cons, etc., etc. And I am well aware how stupid it is; and I thought I was over it when I actually got sentenced to prison ('cause I really really did not want to go). But now that I'm here, I'm starting to embrace my temporary identity as a prisoner (and maybe it's only because I'm here for a short time that I'm able to indulge in this role playing). It's even gotten to the point where I kind of want to stay in Chowchilla and "go over the wall," just so I can experience the more hardcore prison and be able to say I did my term over the wall in Chowchilla. Isn't this all crazy and stupid?! Of course I'm still gonna try to go to CIW (I haven't lost my mind completely), but there is a definite allure about remaining here. But the allure is all based on unexpansive glamorizing/romanticizing of hardcore prison life, which is the same type of glamorizing/romanticizing that got me into all this horrible mess (as well as numerous other messes) in the first place. So I completely understand that G&R-ing [*glamorizing & romanticizing*] these types of non-conformist lifestyles and activities is terribly unproductive, destructive, stupid, equally conformist (as it is seemingly non-conformist), and ultimately unexpansive. And as I mentioned at the beginning of this paragraph, hopefully my renewed indulgence in G&R-ing my current prison status is more of a coping method rather than a regression into old, self-destructive thinking. I mean, if I had a fucking choice, I would most definitely, without a second thought, opt to be free and happily abandon my new found prison identity.

But since that doesn't appear to be anywhere near likely, I may as well approach my stay here as an adventure, as research, an experience to add to my history, give me an unexpected dimension which could make me even more accessible to the public (i.e., appeal/qualify to the more downtrodden of the public, which comprises of the majority of the population, while my education and artistic successes will appeal/qualify to the privileged few). And I may have G&R-ed my "arrival" to prison, but I'm sure that will fade (as it has today, Friday 10/03/08: only my third day here and the "novelty" of being locked in a two-man cell has lost its hardcore charm). I still love to G&R, but truly my genuine G&R-ing is reserved and geared only towards our revolutionary endeavors and our super-formless and ultra-expansive relationship (and of course you and the formation of your rock star/revolutionist icon :)). And the great thing about all this is that being a revolutionary and an artist/musician are all still non-conformist, but our specific revolution and artistic/musical endeavors are all geared toward helping people and this planet, towards the continuous expansion and transcendence of every living being in this world and beyond. So much better than being a criminal, a convict, or a drug addict.

[...] I need to end this so I can mail it today. I'll send you another letter with more info and a visiting request form for you to fill out. I love you dearly, my darling. And I miss you with all my being. I hope you have fun or are having fun (or by the time you get this, had fun) in San Francisco. Good luck and indulge in all the fun and excitement of starting school on Monday—you are gonna kick ass :)!

With Love from a Far Away Place,
Jennifer ☾, R.P.L.

• • •

CCWF (Central California Women's Facility), Chowchilla, CA

Saturday, 10/04/08

My Darling Love — ♥

I miss you. I wish you were here to hold me right now. I had actual nightmares last night, with like ghosts and shit. I can't even recall the last time I had a bona fide nightmare. It's interesting; since I've been incarcerated, I've been dreaming a lot (or at least remembering my dreams because I heard that we dream whenever we're in R.E.M. but we don't always remember them when we wake). It must be that my mind is making up for lack of external and environmental stimulation by creating a vivid dream-life for me when I sleep. This reminds me of a guy I met when I was at Tarzana Treatment Center. He just got out of prison and admitted himself into TTC as a transitional stage to slowly ease himself back into society. I forgot his name but the last four or six years (I can't remember but it was a significant amount of time) of his sentence he served in the S.H.U. (Secure Housing Unit, the hole or solitary confinement, a prison within the prison). Anyway, on one of the times they let him outdoors (because there's a minimum amount of time they must be allowed outdoors: I think it's two or three times a week for half an hour each) he found a leaf that caught his eye and managed to sneak it back with him. So over the course of years, he developed a relationship with this leaf: it was his friend, he talked to it and cared for it and cherished it as if it were his lover or a child. He said it was very odd the things he would do to it and the bond he developed with this leaf. Then one day it either blew away or was destroyed, disintegrated; and he cried over his loss for weeks. When I first heard this story, I thought it was so exceedingly sad yet sweet—it was touching to me. Now I'm reminded of that movie, Castaway, where Tom Hanks develops a similar relationship with a volleyball he names Wilson; and that portrayal makes me think more of madness. I'm wondering if anyone who is forced into solitude, will all of them develop human-like relationships with inanimate objects or does it take a specific type of person already prone to that kind of behavior? Whatever the case may be, I think I'm starting to get seriously affected by being locked in a two-man cell for the majority of the day and evening and all thru the night. I feel bad because I don't think I'm much company for my bunkie, who's an older, French-Dutch-Lebanese lady in her mid-50's (I will tell you more about her later 'cause she's got some interesting stories that are worth discussing). It's just that when I'm depressed or severely under stimulated, I don't feel much like talking. In fact, I think I might prefer being in a cell by myself 'cause all I do is write and sleep, and hopefully read soon once I can get to the library, and masturbate ('cause now I can indulge in that, being in a cell; and it's better if my bunkie's not here so I can really let loose :)). I'm not use to being locked in a cell 'cause I was in the dayroom at County. And it feels like we program less here or at least for shorter increments at a time. And the cells are smaller here than at County: really only one person can be off their bunk at a time. And I don't really have any friends here. I'm weary [*sic*] to make new friends because I don't want to be stuck with them for the long haul if it turns out I don't really like them. And I refuse to approach the two Korean girls in my module. First of all because one of them bugs the shit out of me (I'll tell you why later if I have time); and second because I refuse to make friends or groupings based on ethnicity. So all that I just complained about has informed and influenced my mood and attitude to slight depression and definite lethargy. But I don't want you to worry. It's really not that bad; and I'll adjust and adapt perfectly fine as usual. Plus this two-man cell business will only last like two weeks. Then I'll get moved to an eight-man cell, which is way larger and has an actual window and it's own shower, two sinks, two full-size mirrors, and a toilet with a door! So everything will only get better, especially when I get closer and closer to my parole/release date.

[…] It's now Sunday, 10/05/08; and after I wrote that part in this letter about not having any friends here, the bottom tier programmed (which is me) and I went outside in the yard and inadvertently started making friends. I was standing by myself waiting to go outside and this girl, Julianna, who I secretly think is cool and am slightly attracted to (don't worry not in a lesbo-type of way), yelled over to me, "Hey what are you doing over there standing off to the side by yourself?" And I was like, "I don't know," and casually and very nonchalantly made my way over to her and her friend, Karina, who I also really like. So that was the beginning of me starting to make friends. […] And the other funny thing is that I also ended up talking to that one Korean girl who I said bugged the shit out of me for like 20 minutes while we walked the yard perimeter. Well it was more like she talked the entire time while I listened to her life story. But it was good because I left feeling more compassion for her. And I realized that the reason she is so annoying is because she's not ok with being here in prison (as with nearly all annoying people, she wants to feel loved and she obviously doesn't feel loved, which of course needs to begin with her loving herself). Since she's not comfortable with herself and her environment, she overcompensates, which exhibits itself in highly annoying ways. And I'm also probably more critical and judgmental of her because she's Korean, which is my own personal racial-centric shortcoming. I'm running out of paper so I need to end this letter and spare you from an in depth critique of my seeming racism or biased tendencies against Koreans and even Asians in general.

I love you. I hope to get a letter from you soon. Don't forget about me. Rock out in music school or, rather, transcend the realm of music to that of revolutionary excellence!

I miss you,
Jennifer ☾, R.P.L.

. . .

CCWF (Central California Women's Facility), Chowchilla, CA

Tuesday, 10/07/08

Hello Love — ♥

I'm really starting not to like this period of absolutely no contact with you. And apparently it takes about two weeks for us prisoners to receive incoming mail. Hopefully you've mailed me letters already. As long as I stay in "A" yard, which is receiving, I'm sure they'll find me even if I move houses (plus there's only two other houses I can go to 501 or 502; 504 is for death row and adseg [the jail within the prison], and it's right next door to us so I'm always curious whenever they come out for meals). So send me as many letters as you can. I miss you. I want to be able to hear your voice thru your words, feel your presence, and feel connected to you once again. I miss you, and I'm wondering what you are doing. How's school so far? Tell me your courses and your schedule. Do you like your professors? How are the students? Made any friends yet? And how was your trip to San Francisco?...

[...] So my bunkie, Linda (the 54 year-old French-Dutch-Lebanese lady), has been to Chowchilla before—this is her second time around. This time she's sentenced to two years with half (for what I don't know 'cause I think it's considered rude to ask, but I know she had a co-defendant who's her boyfriend and a Nazi-Lowrider). But last time she was here, she was sentenced to 10 years! She served a little over half: 5 years and 3 or 6 months (the extra months were because she got into a fight when she first got here in Receiving). I'll tell you why she got 10 years later on in this letter because it poses yet another interesting dilemma/issue regarding family values. Anyways, back to this subject. So Linda was telling me that this current sentence (half of two years and also minus about five months in County) is gonna be much harder for her to do than her 10 year sentence because with her 10 year sentence she was resigned to the fact that she was gonna be here for a while. I started thinking about this idea and began relating it to me and how I began thinking about my stay in prison as opposed to jail. […]

Since being in prison, I've noticed that I don't think about you as much as when I was in jail. I think it's the combination of being physically far away from you and having absolutely no contact with you. When I was in Lynwood, I would receive letters from you almost daily, talk to you on the phone a minimum of three or four times a week, and actually see you every weekend. Therefore similar to how my bunkie's view/attitude/feelings of the outside world changed depending on her length of stay in prison, my attachment to you has also changed with my degree of incarceration. Perhaps it will ease you to know that my moods are no longer influenced by whether or not you answer my calls, for example. And if you never write me, I can perhaps easily pretend you don't exist. Being in prison, I feel as if I've been sucked into a black hole, out of existence and into some alternate dimension where its society is comprised of only women wearing bright orange jumpsuits. If I ceased writing you, I could easily forget you and the outside world completely. And in many ways I am more at ease. If you were to run off with some broad, for example, I don't think it would bother me as much as if I were still in County jail. There's something about being in prison—the severity of punishment, the stigma, the degree of isolation and separateness from the outside world, the fact that most of us are here for a minimum of a year with half—that forces one to resign oneself to this alternate prison world and mentality, to assimilate completely to this new reality and forget/let go of all relations with the outside world. And I don't think it's just me. I hardly hear any of the girls here talk about their boyfriends, girlfriends, spouses, lovers, etc. on the outside like I did when I was in County. Yet obviously I'm not letting go of you completely because I'm still writing you constantly. And my current, extreme feelings of separateness and disattachment from you (and hence this seemingly reactionary and nihilistic view of our relationship) is exacerbated by the fact of our abrupt cease of any and all forms of communication. Besides the three or four letters I've written you so far, I have not heard from you in nearly two weeks (it's now Friday, 10/10/08). I'm not saying this is your fault 'cause I know incoming mail takes two weeks to process, and I also initially told you to wait to write until I move to either 502 or 501 (but now I know they'll find me if I move buildings). And the fact is, even though in my waking hours I may not think/worry/fantasize/reminisce about you like I did in jail, my intense attachment to you manifests itself in my dreams when I sleep at night. I love you, my sweet revolutionary darling. And I do hope

I hear from you soon.

I'm gonna end this letter here 'cause I want to put it in the mailbox today. So I'll tell you all about my bunkie in my next letter. She makes an interesting case study and probably, unfortunately represents a significant portion of the population. Even though I said I wouldn't care that much, I hope you're still my R.P.L. (now and for many years to come).

I love you and I miss you tons,
Jennifer ☾, R.P.L.

• • •

CCWF (Central California Women's Facility), Chowchilla, CA

Monday, 10/13/08

Dear Jonathan,

I've been here at Chowchilla now for exactly two weeks and it's really starting to bother me that I haven't received a letter from you yet. I know that it hasn't been two weeks since you've probably mailed me a letter because you had to wait to receive my first letter to know my X# and address. And I hope to friken continuous expansion that you didn't listen to me and started mailing me letters asap. And I know it must be fuckin' hilarious to you that in my last letter I was like "Oh, I'm such a prisoner: I'm so inundated in the prison world, so isolated from the outside that I could care less if you ever thought of me again"—all dramatic and shit. And now I'm all pining away for you: in desperate need for some affirmation that you still love me and are still committed to our relationship. [...] At this moment, I am truly feeling the hurt and pain of separation and absolutely no contact from you and the fear of not knowing how you feel at this moment and the anxiety that you may have found somebody new at music school. Yet it was also true just only a few days ago that I felt secure in my isolation, that I didn't need you, that it wouldn't be the end of the world if I were never to hear or see you again. And all this is exceedingly hilarious to me because I realize the absurdity in my willingness to indulge in extreme emotions such as these. And the truth is (or what I'd like to be the truth is) that I love you, I miss you, I hope to get a letter from you soon; and if you do end up falling in love with another at music school, at least it'll make good material for my movie (and I get to be right that love will always tragically allude me in some overly dramatic and romanticized way). [...]

[...] I just received my very first letter in prison. When the C.O. called my name for mail, I got so excited (especially since I just wrote how I'm concerned that I haven't received a letter from you yet) thinking it was a letter from you. But it wasn't. It was a letter from my mom, which was highly disappointing. The letter was fucking thick, which surprised me; but I soon found out why. It was filled with letters from Colin—my mom only wrote one page, front side only. I hope I get a letter from you soon 'cause I can't be left with these letters from Colin. They were so sad, I had to hold back tears. They were full of apologies, feelings of guilt, regret, expressions of love, and visions of a future he knows will never happen. I know you are not interested in the details but at one point he writes how he has recently been having nightmares of me being involved with another man. He wants to know if I've met someone else. I suppose I need to tell him 'cause I would want to know (and as you had said, it'll help him let go); but then again, I'm not facing the dismal future he is. God, I wish you would write me (or better, I hope I get one of your letters soon). I'm feeling quite sad so I'm gonna end this letter here. I love you and I hope you still love me too... I hope nothing has changed.

Missing You in My Life,
Jennifer, R.P.L.

• • •

CCWF (Central California Women's Facility), Chowchilla, CA

Friday, 10/17/08

My Dearest Love — ♥

I finally received your first letters (the one you initially mailed to Lynwood and added onto after you received my shoebox) two days ago—the day after I mailed you that sad letter. And I got your second letter yesterday. Your letters came just in time. Thank continuous expansion (I've decided I'm gonna start saying this whenever one of the multitude of prisoners says to me, "Thank the Lord" or "Praise Jesus"—maybe I'll also add, "Praise 3CE"). It was so good to read your letters and feel your presence in my life again. […]

[…] I really miss you right now. I actually feel like crying. I think I may have been happier in the 2-man cell. Everyone in my current cell is really nice but being around 7 other women nearly 24 hours each and everyday has made me feel even more different and separate. I have noticed I've become quieter, more secluded in my own mind, not wanting to talk and participate. I didn't really talk much with my bunkie in the 2-man cell but at least I could get lost in my Bridging and writing letters to you. Here in the 8-man cell, there are so many personalities and the socialization of prison and the dramas are now in my face, in my house. Don't get me wrong, it's highly entertaining and I laugh a lot but as an on-looker & only on the side-lines. Even though I don't feel a part of, I still get very distracted by all of it. […] But I don't want you to worry about me. I will never be defeated completely. I want you to concentrate fully on music school, which brings me back to the subject I really rather discuss. I will be just fine, my darling. I just love you so very much...

[…] It's now Monday, 10/20/08 (yesterday, the 19th, was my 7 months!). I should have mailed you a quick, little letter the day I got your first letter on Wednesday so you don't worry, having left you with that sad, depressing letter. I apologize. […] Thank you for writing me, my love. It makes a world of difference when I receive letters from you. I am grateful everyday for your love.

I also want you to know that I'm feeling less lonely and socially awk-ward. I no longer feel so much like a social outcast anymore. […] I think the reason why I was feeling especially alone and separate this past Saturday (the day I wrote that one part of this letter) is because I offered too much of myself (or rather, my beliefs/values) too soon, without waiting for the invitation. So Sheila, the stud-broad, was talking about how during part of her 5 year prison term she made a decision to walk with the Lord and not fuck around with women. So I didn't hold back this time and asked her if she's not allowed to be gay and also walk with the Lord. Of course every single one of my cellmates are Christian and the most hardcore of them and Sheila began saying shit. And I was all geared up to go too, ready to de-bate (I don't know what got into me: I think I was getting antsy 'cause our program got canceled because there was a fight so we were stuck with each other in our cell for over 24 hours; and I had been basically quiet, keeping to myself until then, since Tuesday). But Smiley, our resident prison ex-pert who's currently doing a 6 year term, shut it down immediately saying, "Uh-uh, we're not doing this here." She wasn't mean or anything but I still felt dismissed and even more separate and different from my cellies. And that's when I wrote how much I missed you and how lonely I was feeling. But now everything's great. Saturday night I got in a bit of a heated debate with the most hardcore Christian, Laura; but it provided a forum for me to articulate ideas of continuous expansion and revolution to the rest of my cellies who had no choice but to listen. And then Sunday mid-morning I engaged in a kind and loving way with Laura for quite some time and again for the rest of my cellies to indirectly listen to. By Sunday late afternoon, I gained enough respect and peaked enough interest thru my interactions with Laura that Sheila, the stud who is definitely the biggest personality in my cell, began asking me about the revolution. And even Smiley started coming over to my bunk to talk (not about revolution or anything), but I think it's more because she likes my chi-chi's (i.e., my boobs :)). Now even though my cellies joke and poke fun at me about the revolution, I can tell they respect me. Sheila last night said, while we were waiting to go to dinner, "I don't know about Moon over there and the revolution. She's gonna be a star and I'm gonna say I was in the pen with that broad." And then she asked, "How many people you got for the revolution?... Don't tell me it's just you and that R.P.L.!" And I just bust out laughing because it's true.

[…] I love you, my dearest R.P.L. And I miss you more than you'll ever know (actually you probably do know because I tell you all the time). I am so fuckin' hungry right now. Praise 3CE that it's almost dinner time. The food is significantly better here but they definitely don't feed us enough. And they're suppose to give us 15 minutes to eat but they never do. I have never eaten so fast in my life! Ok, I really gotta go now or this letter won't go out tomorrow. I love you!!

You are the absolute best,
Jennifer ☾, R.P.L.

. . .

CCWF (Central California Women's Facility), Chowchilla, CA

Thursday, 10/23/08

My Dearest Jonathan — ♥

[…] This morning at breakfast Smiley and her crew, Kiki and Baby, schooled me on being too generous with my stuff (i.e., canteen items like food). I explained to them that since I know my parents are gonna take care of me, I don't mind sharing with people who aren't so fortunate. Smiley said that's fine and great but I gotta draw the line somewhere or else they'll take everything I have and then laugh at me behind my back for being a punk. I then tried to explain that I'm not tied to material goods and if people wanna laugh at me, they can go ahead because I know that I am ultimately more expansive for not being a capitalist and also for being loving. Then Kiki said, "Ok check this out. If you just give your stuff away easy like that, the next time you shop and you don't buy as much, those bitches will just take your shit." Smiley continued by reminding me that I'm in prison and that unfortunately things go down like that—I have to remember where I am. I know Smiley and her crew are looking out for me, but I don't want to compromise my values and beliefs just because I'm in prison. I think I can be generous and respected at the same time. I can be sweet, kind, loving, and even Pollyanna-like and also not be a punk. I'm fairly confident that I will not be taken advantage of and that I will most definitely fight back if I have to. As Sheila said in reply to our new cellie being in shock that I use to shoot heroin, "Oh Moon over there's a gansta. She ain't no joke." So I'll keep giving my shit away if people ask for it because if they're asking for it, then they obviously feel they need it; and I never need anything that bad where I feel the need to hoard it, especially material goods.

[...] Regarding the Presidential debate and pop politics, I would be pleased if Obama was elected just for the simple fact that he is a person of color. And I would be similarly pleased if Clinton had won because she's a woman. I know it seems very racial- and sex-centric, which it is. But to me, the realm of pop politics is an illusion for change—it does nothing but reinforce and perpetuate the current oppressive/repressive paradigms, which are in place. And the only function of pop politics is as a realm for the public to feel they are making a difference, to feel socio-politically responsible, to feel smart and informed. It is just another tool of capitalism designed to perpetuate itself, yet disguised and presented as the opposite—it is presented as the only place where significant change can occur. For this reason I have never been invested in pop politics. However this election year is different. And I will only be interested if Obama is elected because it will show a shift in this country's collective consciousness if they are to elect a person of color for President. So in a way, for me, pop politics—much like pop culture—is simply a tool to gauge the "minute strata of demographics" in this country. But I definitely agree with you (not that I was disagreeing with you or opposing you in my last sentence) that the candidates (i.e., individual people) are not to blame—it is more the manner in which the over-arching structures of news media, television, and communication in general are "moving toward sound-bytes and sensationalism," as you say. This is why it is so imperative that we utilized and control these powerful and highly influential tools (i.e., television, internet, radio, newspapers, magazines, etc.) for the revolution—it is in fact necessary. And again, I'm sure you already know all this.

[…] They just passed out mail and no mail for me. It's been a week since I received your last letter. I hope you are ok. Unless we get re-routed mail later tonight after dinner and one of the letters is yours, then I'm gonna have to wait 'til Monday. I hope you wrote me. Again I hope you are okay. And now my insecurities are resurfacing and I'm hoping you haven't replaced me for another. But it's good to know I'm not the only one who goes thru crazy, irrational thoughts. One of my cellies, Rochelle, hasn't received mail from her man yet and she's been here a week and a half, and she's starting to freak. She keeps saying, "Once I start getting mail, I'll be all right." I'll just concentrate on my Bridging this weekend. I hope everything is good with you.

It's almost dinner so I'm gonna say goodbye for now. I was gonna comment more on the intro to our text that you so eloquently wrote but that's gonna have to wait 'til later. I just reread the last paragraph to your third letter and it reassured me that you still love me. I love when I dream about you while I sleep (even though many of the dreams are unpleasant) because when I wake I feel like I just spent time with you. I can't wait to be with you again.

I LOVE YOU,
Your R.P.L.,
Jennifer ☾

. . .

CCWF (Central California Women's Facility), Chowchilla, CA

Wednesday, 10/29/08

Hello My Love — ♥

I just met with my counselor today. My release date is 5/20/09. According to my calculations, I'm actually serving about 9 ½ months! I was sentenced on 8/18/08 so from that date to 5/20/09 is 9 months and 2 days, plus the 2 weeks I served in county when I was initially arrested to the time my parents bailed me out would make it a little over 9 ½ months. According to my face sheet, I only got 61 days credit from county: 42 days post-sentence + 17 + 2 (I'm assuming the 17 are the days when I was in county from my initial arrest and the 2 are my good time/work time credits from the 17). So it seems I didn't get good time/work time credits for the time I was in Lynwood after my sentencing because it took me 6 weeks to catch the chain (arrived 9/30/08), which is 42 days. I thought I was gonna get around 90 days (3 months) credit from county with good time/work time, which would make my release date a month earlier, toward the end of April. But whatever, it's only a month longer than I thought. Actually, that's not right because 3 months minus 18 months is 15 months. Half of 15 is 7 ½ and 7 ½ months from 9/30/08 is like the 15th of May, which is about my current release date (5/20/09). So obviously I don't know how to calculate the time because using the same formula with my actual credits would be 61 days or 2 months minus 18 months is 16 months. Half of 16 is 8 and 8 months from 9/30/08 is like the 1st of June. I guess it's all around the same date, give or take 5-10 days. I don't know. I guess it doesn't really matter all that much. Sheila thinks they calculated my credits wrong, which she swears sometimes happens, and that once I go over the wall and see my counselor there, I'll get a new release date. I'm not counting on that though. My face sheet says 5/20/09 is my release date (actually, it's my minimum release date) so that's what I'm going by. My maximum release date, which is the date if I were to serve my entire 18 month sentence, is 1/07/10. Thank continuous expansion I don't have to serve my whole sentence!

[…] The last I heard from you was your letter written 10/15 and 10/19. In that letter you said you were "ungodly sick." I haven't heard from you since so I'm a bit worried. I held off from mailing this letter yesterday (Wednesday, 10/29) to see if I get a letter from you today so that I don't end this letter in an unnecessary worried note. I hope I get a letter from you today (Thursday, 10/30) because my mind will automatically start thinking you're dead. […] Today during our morning program, I told my friend, Lisa, "I think my R.P.L. is dead." At first she was all concerned asking, "Why?!" But then after I explained to her why, she laughed at me and said, "You are stupid!" But at least I'm not as bad as Lisa. Lisa's wife, Alicia, didn't write or Lisa didn't get a letter from Alicia in like three days, maybe four at the most, and fuckin' Lisa wrote a horrible letter to her wife saying shit like, "You fucking bitch, why aren't you writing me?... What are you doing out there?... Are you fucking around on me?!" I told Lisa she was being crazy and over-reacting and that maybe she should write Alicia another letter apologizing and explaining her feelings and her needs/desires. Lisa's response was "She should be writing me everyday just so I know she's not fuckin' around on me out there." I don't know, Jonathan. These "bitches" in here are kind of crazy. So much revolves around what bitch is going with what bitch, who's wife is who's, this bitch is my girl but this other bitch is my wife, etc., etc. And there have been so many fights. Some of it's over girls, but I think more of them have been over issues of disrespect: "calling someone out of their name," as they say, which is basically a perceived disrespectful tone when addressing someone. But back to my friend, Lisa. She constantly talks and complains about her wife, Alicia. Saying stuff like, "I don't know if I can do this," meaning her relationship with Alicia. But then yesterday Lisa gets Alicia's name tattooed on her leg! Women in prison seem to become exaggerated, caricatured stereotypes of themselves. And I don't know about getting a prison tattoo, especially on "A" yard. At least when you go over the wall, you can get actual tattoo ink and they make tattoo guns out of tape cassette players. But in Receiving, on "A" yard, they use a staple as a needle and crushed pencil lead mixed with soap as ink! I don't know about that, but apparently it stays. And to be honest, whoever did Lisa's tattoo actually did a decent job: it's simple but the handwriting is exceedingly neat and perfect looking.

[...] Mail came and went. No mail from you. Now I'm really worried. Please be okay. My previous letters haven't upset you in any way? For a split second, I contemplated the possibility of you being mad or annoyed at me. What I wanted to say in regards to Lisa and all the prison bitches, that I forgot to say, is that when I listen to Lisa and many of the women here, I am always grateful of the relationship I share with you—that our relationship is not based on possessive love and expectations. I love you, Jonathan. I hope your health is better and that everything is good in your life. Write soon, okay?

LOVE,
Jennifer ♥, R.P.L.

• • •

CCWF (Central California Women's Facility), Chowchilla, CA

Saturday, 11/01/08

My Darling Jonathan — ♥

I received your letter that you wrote on the back of the Norman Mailer correspondences from the New Yorker yesterday, Friday, Halloween. Thank you!

[. . .] I don't know anything about Norman Mailer except that his name is familiar. The primary thought(s) I was left with after reading the article revolved around confirmation of my disinterest in what I call "pop politics" (stated this way in reference to Mailer's letter to Sal Cetrano on 3/28/99: "...While the Democrats...disgust me with what I call their 'boutique politics'..."—because I know you are already familiar with my concept of pop politics). It just struck me, the ending—how the last two paragraphs of the last letter included in the article had such a despairing "world doom" view of the future. My personal belief is that Mailer's close involvement and interest in the unexpansive, devoid-of-its-original-meaning (or any significant or innovative or insightful meaning at that), and exceedingly-informed-by-Capitalism realm of pop politics (much in parallel with pop culture, hence the name) caused much of Mailer's over-arching bouts of depression, despair, and lack of confidence in himself and the world. You have said this to me many times that in order to change or destroy something, one cannot use the very thing one is fighting against in an attempt to destroy it. One cannot fight violence with violence, as you have said many times. It is clear that Mailer was a Communist at one point and maintained an anti-Capitalism position throughout. Yet he was unable to make any headway because of his close ties and interests in pop politics: Mailer's paradigms in which his thinking subscribed was informed or at least heavily influenced by pop politics, which in turn is informed by Capitalism. Even as an artist, a writer, Mailer's novel revolved around the CIA. In order to successfully destroy, dismantle, change and offer an alternative to Capitalism and other oppressive/repressive structures, systems, paradigms, we need to exist, operate, and approach from a realm at the furthest reaches of Capitalism and oppression/repression (nothing really exists outside the reaches and influences of Capitalism, which is why I say the realm furthest from its insidious grasp). This is why I engage in and herald fantasy so much. This is why I love the X-Men and New Mutants, Star Trek: The Next Generation, and even gaudy, cheesy songs like "Greatest Love of All" and "Magic." Fantasy is the realm to approach the revolution from. Of course I still believe in utilizing the same tools Capitalism uses, like pop culture, corporations, the education system—and we may even have a representative in pop politics—but I will always back it up by saying, "This is all towards a future as depicted in Star Trek: The Next Generation," or something to that effect, even though as you had once noted, I sound crazy when I say shit like that. You may not agree with me whole-heartedly or maybe not at all; but both of us being artists and also the ones to herald the revolution is not without significance.

I agree with Mailer when he wrote Eiichi Yamanishi on 10/23/61, "By this I do not mean that Marxism no longer applies but only that for it to become exciting again as a style of thought for the best of the young people it must be expanded by some genius who can comprehend the complexities of the American phenomena." I truly and sincerely believe we are the geniuses Mailer is referring to. Do you feel the same? I have felt this way since 1993-94 (though back then I fell into delusions of grandeur, believing I was the second coming or prophet savior of the world), and I feel this way today; and I hope I die an ungodly death before I relinquish my faith and assurance in myself, in you (my dear dear R.P.L.), and the world. Do I sound overly dramatic and somewhat gaudy? Good, god-fuckin'-dammit! And that's how I'm stayin'! [...]

I agree with Mailer again in the same letter to Eiichi Yamanishi on 10/23/61: "The difficulty here in America is that the conventional forms of revolutionary Marxism simply do not apply to the peculiarly intricate structure of American society." This I think is very true, which is why I never say I'm a Marxist and rarely say I'm a communist or socialist (unless in a hurried oppositional remark/stance against Capitalism). That book, Capitalism for Beginners, explores the various reasons why Socialism has never flourished in America. [...] Mailer touched on it a bit when he wrote, "...the difficulty is that the working class in America is utterly without a revolutionary consciousness..." (letter to Eiichi Yamanishi, 10/23/61) and "...there are political phenomena in America which Marx could never have contemplated, for the continued survival of capitalism displaced the economic imbalance into a psychic imbalance which corrupts the very being of people's lives here" (letter to Eiichi, 4/17/64). There are other interesting conclusions and insights Mailer writes in his correspondences; but I fear this letter is beginning to resemble an essay consisting primarily of quotes, so I'm gonna end here. I hope these sorts of ramblings don't bore or annoy you in their seeming and somewhat redundancy and repetition of ideas.

There is so much more I want to write (mostly in response to the things you wrote in your letter) but it's getting late and there was a huge blow out in my cell revolving around Shurita (or Rita or Shea for short) or as Sheila calls her Special #2 or Funkadelics (because Rita emits heavy amounts of body odor, though she showers daily). Special #1 is my bunkie, Diane, who I often feel sorry for but also confused and unsure of her level of awareness. My cell has just recently gotten crazy with the yelling fights between Rita and Rochelle. But it can also be exceedingly funny, which I think is mostly Sheila's doing. Sheila's great. She looks like a hard, mean "nigga" (as she would say) or stud-broad (as I would say), but she's actually very sweet and has an amazing sense of humor, which I think comes from a heightened awareness and insight of human behavior. Anyways, it really got crazy-style in here with Rita yelling and talking ceaselessly and going off on some diatribe and then Rochelle, who has an incredibly loud and ear-splitting voice, screaming on top of Rita's non-stop, one-woman, floor performance. And then me trying to interject in a compassionate and loving way during one of the split-second lulls in noise eruption, which only got Rita going strong again. Until finally Sheila exclaimed, "You, 2 Up [which is my bed #], if you start again with your revolution talk when Special #2's all done and shut-up, I'm gonna have to get up on you!" Sheila's so funny. She can always manage to lighten a tense situation and make us all laugh in the end. [...]

[...] I wanted to say one more thing relating to the Norman Mailer correspondences. The reason I got all crazy-style, ornery, and defensive-like regarding my belief in fantasy and the belief we are the geniuses to herald the revolution is because I have an enormous fear that I will end up like Mailer: disillusioned, discouraged with no hope or faith in the world. I had quite a few people tell me while I was in school that I'm still young and naive and once I get older and live life more, my thinking, values and beliefs will change and I will abandon these child-like notions relating to continuous expansion. I was always quick and adamant to say, "That'll never happen to me!" And so far it hasn't. I want to be like Mailer's friend, James Jones, who "...loves life so instinctively and so warmly" (letter to Lewis Allen, 4/30/54). Mailer in a previous letter to Charley and Jill Devlin on the same day, 4/30/54, describes Jonesie as "...very complex, very noisy, very crude, very affectionate, amazing you first with his naïveté and then with his shrewdness and insight." Very alluring and seductive, indeed. Yet truly, Jonathan, please kill me if I ever abandon the revolution or pursuit of continuous expansion.

[…] I need to end this letter because, once again, it's nearly lights out. I want to apologize for putting so much pressure on you to write me more. It's more important for you to concentrate on school. Receiving a letter from you about once a week is just fine with me. I love you, Jonathan, and I miss you very very much. I look forward to a visit (a contact visit!) and the day I get released to you...

With All My Love (and delight in you),
Jennifer ☾, R.P.L.

• • •

CCWF (Central California Women's Facility), Chowchilla, CA

Friday, 11/07/08

Hello My Dearest Love — ♥

Sorry I haven't written in a while—in about a week. I've been feeling—how do they say it in AA?—restless, irritable, and discontent. This past week, I have felt so over "A" yard. I'm so done with Receiving: I just want to move on to my permanent location. I want my damn quarterly package and my friken typewriter! I have not wanted to do anything this week. I'm sick of Bridging so I didn't really work on that, leaving me even further behind (I'm still working on the second packet: Week 2). I'm sick of hand-writing so I didn't write you any letters (once again, I apologize). […]

[…] I went on a tangent for a few pages. The original intention of this letter (besides reminding you that I love you and I miss you :)) is to let you know that I'm transpacking early this coming week (either Monday, Tuesday, or Wednesday). Transpacking means I'm not going over the wall here at Chowchilla. I don't know exactly where I'm going because they won't tell us for security reasons; but I'm hoping it's CIW. All my property is already boxed and shipped—we did that yesterday, Friday (it's now Saturday, 11/08/08). As I've told you before, everyone here, meaning prisoners (because C.O.'s are not very helpful), swear by varying information so it's difficult to know what's true. This is what I think. When one gets a transpacking ducat, it means she's either going to Live Oak or CIW. When one gets a transfer ducat, it means she's going across the street to VSP. Girls going over the wall don't get ducats: they are simply given muumuus 10 minutes before they go. I got a transpacking ducat so I'm thinking I'm going to CIW because I told my counselor that I absolutely do not want to go to Live Oak. And since I'm obviously not staying in Chowchilla, which was my second choice, I'm assuming or safely hoping that I'm headed for CIW. I'll know more certainly by the day I leave. If I get a ducat Sunday night to leave Monday, it means I'm going to Live Oak (which if that happens, I think I'll cry). If I get a ducat to leave Tuesday, many girls believe it means one is going across the street to VSP (but I still think it's a transfer ducat not a transpacking ducat one gets to go across the street 'cause that's how it went with two of the girls in my cell the day after I moved into 501). The consensus regarding CIW is that if one gets a ducat Tuesday night to leave early Wednesday morning at 5:30 am, it means she's going to CIW. So obviously I'm hoping for a ducat Tuesday night. But I'm not gonna assume anything until I actually set foot in whatever facility I'm going to. But at least I'm going somewhere. If you remember at the beginning of this letter, I was complaining about wanting to go. This past week only, I've been hating being here in Receiving; so my transpacking ducat came just in time. Isn't it great how that worked. It actually took me the shortest amount of time to go through Receiving: 6 weeks (on Tuesday, 11/11/08). So including the 6 weeks I was in county, I've been locked up for about 3 months. Only 6 more months to go. That's half a year. It sounds better as 6 months. I've done a third of my sentence. Only two more sessions like I just did and then I'm out. I can do that. […]

[…] By the unexpansive components of the 3CE, my new bunkie is completely blowing me up with her incessant and highly pungent farts!! It is seriously bad. And I'm on the top bunk so it rises and then lingers, trapped by the ceiling and the wall next to me. Thank continuous expansion that I'm leaving within the next few days (it's now Sunday, 11/09/08) because her gassy emissions are horrendously foul. Did you know that the average smell weighs 760 nanograms? I learned this fact from a magazine called PLM (Prison Living Magazine). […]

[…] Well, I did not get a ducat tonight so I'm not leaving tomorrow, Monday. That's good, I think. Though one of my cellies thinks they go to CIW on Monday because Orange County comes up on Monday, and she thinks they drop us off at CIW on their way back. I shouldn't listen to Wendy though because she's a newbie: she's never been to prison before. Yet she does sound hella convincing. You know, I've never experienced such a lack of factual information or plethora of varying, sometimes opposite information, presented as facts as I have in prison. What's that all about? I have a guess or a theory but not the time or energy nor the paper (this is my last piece) to indulge. It has to do with the social structure and identity formation of the prisoner, though.

I miss you, Jonathan. I hope you are happy and in good health and inspired. As with you, your letters bring me joy so I hope I get another real soon. And I hope by Wednesday, I'll be closer to you physically...

I love you,
Your R.P.L.,
Jennifer ☾

. . .

Part III: Acclimation

"Learning to love yourself, it is the greatest love of all."
Whitney Houston

Thursday, 11/13/08

Dearest Jonathan — ♥

As the return address on the envelope indicates, I did not end up at CIW (or CI Wonderful as many prisoners affectionately call it: as I understand it, CIW was the first prison opened so there are a lot of old-timer lifers there—the Manson girls are at CIW. Thought you might find that little bit of trivia somewhat interesting). I ended up being transported directly across the street to VSP (Valley State Prison), an option that was not discussed or even mentioned when meeting with my counselor (we talked about CIW, Live Oak, and Chowchilla but no VSP). But supposedly that happens quite often—"they just ship you where ever there's room," as I've heard about twenty times. So my question is, why do they even ask you where you'd like to go if it's really not gonna make a difference? Yet to be fair, I did make a big stink about not wanting to go to Live Oak, which thank continuous expansion I didn't end up there because apparently it's more like 4-6 hours further north from Chowchilla, and I did make it clear that Chowchilla was my second choice; so I suppose they could have figured that since VSP is just across the street, it's basically the same thing as Chowchilla. And VSP is set-up identical to Chowchilla in terms of the layout (VSP was built after Chowchilla and the rumor is that the state plans to build two more identical prisons so that there's a prison on all four corners—just what this world needs, more prisons). I hope you get my following analogy because I thought it was quite humorous and clever but no one got it (and I sadly tried it out on three separate audiences). I said, "VSP is like Bizarro World Chowchilla." Please tell me you know what Bizarro World is because I had to explain it to all three people/groups I made the comment to, which made it significantly less funny (I guess I'm probably one of the only comic book geeks in this joint, though it could also be a generational/age issue seeing as most of the people I told it to were younger than me). You probably won't think it's funny either because I think you also need to have been to both places to really see the humor. The only person who found it mildly humorous (after, of course, having to explain what Bizarro World is) was DC, the token ultra-stud in my new cell, only because he (I say he instead of she because it's difficult to not think of them as boys when they look exactly like boys) spent his first three years at Chowchilla. So in case you don't know what Bizarro World is, let me quickly explain. In the DC Superman comic books, Superman enters a parallel universe, nearly identical to his own, a mirror image except for some minute differences. There is even another Superman in this parallel universe, which DC comics calls Bizarro World. I don't know the details of the Superman Bizarro World, but I thought it was a common notion: Seinfeld even used it for one of his sitcom episodes. Anyways, so VSP is a mirror image of Chowchilla except for minor differences like, the C.O.'s in Chowchilla ride around on bicycles with three wheels while here at VSP the C.O.'s ride normal bicycles with two wheels (same cruiser-style bikes in both places though). And "A" Yard at Chowchilla is completely empty besides a volleyball net while VSP "A" Yard has bleachers, tables with stools, and a workout area with pull-up bars and inclined slats for sit-ups—the grass is greener here at VSP too. There are other small differences like, the tile pattern and color and the type of door for the bathroom and shower, but on a larger scale it is identical, a mirror-image, of Chowchilla. The main difference between the two sister prisons, which many people have told me, is that Chowchilla is run by the prisoners while VSP is run by the C.O.'s: VSP is rumored to be more structured than Chowchilla. The most significant difference I noticed immediately, along with all the other transfer prisoners from Chowchilla, is that we get more food here. Usually I clean off every morsel from my tray and am still hungry, but last night and this morning at VSP I actually gave away food and still had some left on my tray. This is a very good thing because it certainly is a sad (and tense) state of affairs for everyone to be hungry all of the time.

I was finally processed into VSP and housed last night (Wednesday, 11/12/08) around 8 pm. The only reason I wished I could have stayed at Chowchilla was to avoid the entire, long and tedious, and exceedingly annoying receiving process. We arrived at VSP around 11 am and didn't get housed, as I said, until 8 pm: that's nine hours of sitting in a holding tank (and that's not counting the two hours sitting in a holding tank at Chowchilla). If I stayed at Chowchilla, I wouldn't have to be processed all over again (which involves the horrible strip searches where we have to squat and cough several times and then bend over, spread our vaginas open and cough until they see our vaginal muscles move—and we had to do this twice, once when we left Chowchilla and then again when we got to VSP) because I would be staying in the same prison: I would simply be going over the wall to one of the main yards, either B, C, or D. And let me tell you, the state sure approaches the transporting of prisoners fairly seriously. Coming up from Lynwood, they only handcuffed one of our hands to another prisoner's with a fairly lengthy chain—they didn't even link us all together with one super long chain like when they take us to court. But yesterday, just to transport us across the street, they put a chain around our waist, handcuffed both our hands to the chain around our waist so we couldn't really lift up our hands, and then they shackled our feet together so we can only take small steps. And if that wasn't enough, they had a dude sitting in a caged area in the back with a shotgun between his legs. They really don't want us to escape; and even if we did manage to get away, they have us dressed in over-sized, polka-dot muumuus, which I'm sure everyone in this area recognizes as prison garb.

I'm okay with the fact that I'm at VSP now; but let me tell you, I was seriously hoping—and, at times, even convinced—that I was still going to CIW. Even after we pulled into VSP, I desperately thought that maybe they're only dropping some of us off here and the rest of us were going back down with them to CIW (because I knew that bus came up from Chino and was going back down after VSP). And even now, a part of me can still rationalize that I'm really endorsed to go to CIW because this one girl in my old cell at Chowchilla went over the wall but she was really endorsed to go to Live Oak. I guess there wasn't space at the time in Live Oak so she had to go over the wall and wait for some indeterminable amount of time. So, of course, a part of me thinks this is my case too. I'm stupid though because I know this is most likely not my case (see, I can't even say it's not my case—I have to add, most likely). You should have heard me the night before when I got my ducat and it said I was leaving at 10 am instead of 5:30 am. I kept asking about five of the same questions over again in different ways and rationalizing out loud that I possibly could still be going to CIW. Finally, after telling me about twenty times that I'm going to VSP, Rochelle said, "Ok Boo, you're going to CIW." I went a little CIW-crazy there for a minute; but only because I was convinced that I was going there. Yet I should always remember that usually when I insist on something being true, it generally isn't (I've known this about myself for over a decade but somehow I always manage to forget, especially at the time). It's okay though. Ultimately it doesn't matter where I do my time—a prison's a prison. The only real reason I want to be at CIW is because I figured I'd get more visits from you. Though I know you'll still visit me here, just not as often and as easily.

The good part is that I seem to have been put in a good room. I don't think any of my cellies are lifers (not that there's anything wrong with lifers) and none of them seem to be overly controlling and freakish about things like hair on the floor or the wool blankets or water in the sink, etc. The closest one to being that way is probably my bunkie (I can't remember her name). This morning when I was brushing my teeth, she said as nice as possible, "You can brush your teeth over the sink." I tried to explain that I brush my teeth for a few minutes so I move out of the way in case anyone else needs to use the sink. It turned out that I was brushing my teeth near her mug (with a lid) that was on the table next to the sinks and she was concerned I might spray toothpaste and saliva all over her cup—though I've not ever seen anyone do such a thing when brushing her/his teeth. And apparently, every morning she gets on her hands and knees and wipes down the floor, the lockers, and the walls in our area because "[she's] a woman and knows how to take care of [herself]." Anyways, I don't want to sound like I'm complaining or talking ill of my bunkie. I just think it's funny or interesting when prisoners are obviously overly-clean and try to enforce it or at least make it apparent to everyone around them: it just seems they are over-compensating for something. Though I shouldn't talk because I'm O.C.D.-like about shit too; but I think it's different somehow. For one thing, I try to hide my O.C.D. as much as possible. Yet it probably all still comes down to a similar issue: an issue of control in one way or another—whether it's control of other people or control of how someone perceives you or an attempt to control the various particles around you.

[…] I want to get this letter in the mail and it's almost dinner, so I'm gonna say goodbye for now. I love you and I'm looking forward to a letter (and hopefully a visit soon too).

Sending you love, kisses, and hugs from a new faraway place,
Jennifer ☾, R.P.L.

• • •

VSPW (Valley State Prison for Women), Chowchilla, CA

Saturday, 11/15/08

Hello My Love — ♥

It's Saturday and I just tried to sign-up to use the phone this morning for one of the fifteen minute slots between 11 am and noon: I tried to do it legally this time. But apparently the varying information (often mis-information) presented as facts syndrome, which I described in one of my more recent letters, runs among the C.O.'s as well. When I first arrived in my housing unit at VSP, one of the C.O.'s (a regular-staff C.O. too, as opposed to an off-staff C.O., meaning a C.O. who doesn't usually work in our unit) told us that unclassified inmates, which is me, are allowed one phone call a month (all classified inmates are allowed one, or maybe even two, phone call(s) everyday). But when I went up to the cop shop to sign-up for the phone, the other C.O. said unclassified inmates can't make phone calls at all. So that blew my plan. But I go to classification this coming Thursday (I already got my ducat to get classified) so I should be able to call next Saturday. I will try to call you during first unlock, which today first unlock was around 11 am. But I think first unlock is usually earlier because my cellies were acting like we should've been out already around 10 am. But I don't know. In any case, I will try to call you sometime before noon so if you can be at home Saturday morning, I would surely appreciate it. Or you can try putting money on your cell phone so I can call you whenever. It doesn't really matter all that much either way—I kind of gotten use to not being able to talk to you.

[…] I'm actually quite content here at VSP though. As I've already mentioned in my last letter, I have a really good room. And it just got a little bit better or at least a lot more relaxed and comfortable. I was wrong when I told you we didn't have any lifers in our cell. My bunkie, K-Luv (the one I wrote about in my last letter who I couldn't remember her name), is a lifer. She's been down for thirteen years now. Wow, I can't even imagine. So I understand why she's a tad controlling or somewhat over-bearing and overly-concerned with cleanliness. It seems like it's primarily the lifers that are this way. K-Luv is actually kind of mellow compared to all the horror stories of some rooms/lifers I heard about on A yard. And K-Luv has been really nice to me. Yet some of the other girls in my room apparently had issues with her. I said "had" because K-Luv is no longer my bunkie nor in this room anymore. No one knows why she was made to move but most of my cellies, especially Rachel, rejoiced at her departure. Now everyone in my cell is a short-timer (long-timers are 10 years or more). Actually I think Adela has 10 years but she's mellow and fun. Everyone in my cell has a date though, meaning everyone has a parole date as opposed to lifers who have no date. Since K-Luv's leaving, my room has become noticeably more at ease, relaxed, and fun. My new bunkie's another short-timer who just came over the wall from VSP A yard and who is actually paroling before me. Rachel's been here for about two years and has two more years to go. DC's been down for three years, I think, and is paroling August of next year. I don't know how long Lori's been here but I don't think that long and she's paroling just before me, I think in March. Christina just arrived too, the same day I did but from over the wall like my bunkie (I learned that people from up north do their Receiving at VSP and people from down south, like me, do Receiving at Chowchilla; so most people at VSP are from up north), and she's paroling in April. I don't know how long Twin's been here or when she's leaving but according to Lori, Twin's a short-timer too. And I've already told you about Adela who's the only long-timer, just barely with ten years; and I think she just got here recently too, though she's been to prison a lot before. So those are all of my cellies and they are all very nice. After being moved, K-Luv was trying to get back in our room so she was asking everyone if they wanted to move. When she got to me, DC yelled out, "Moon's not leaving," which felt exceedingly nice to be wanted. And I seemed to have melded socially to my room a lot quicker than my last room (if you remember, I wrote all about how it takes me a while to be accepted into new social groups/environments/situations). So because I have such a great room, I don't mind doing my time here at VSP. I just hope you still come visit me. I also can't wait for Thursday so I'll know for sure what's up—with everything, not just where I'm endorsed but what kind of job I'll get, if I have to do the SAP (drug treatment) program, etc.

It's a lot different here on one of the main yards (I'm on C yard) than on A yard or Receiving. For one thing, Monday thru Friday everyone programs, meaning they either work or go to school (once they're classified that is); so everyone's gone most of the day. And almost all the cells have at least one TV: we have two TV's, three when K-Luv was here, which makes the cells feel more homey. In my cell on A yard, my whole room (except me) would basically sleep all day because we would rarely be let out and there's only so much reading and writing one can do. But here on the main yard, many people have been here for years and years so there's a much different vibe. People are in a groove, they have their life established here in prison: they have their job (or school), they go out to the yard, have their social groups, their girlfriends/wives, their projects/scams/hustles, etc., etc. People are busy in prison. People are so established here that I feel self-conscious and hyper-aware of my loner status. On A yard, everyone's new again (though many are not first-timers) so it didn't feel so strange to me that I hung out by myself—it didn't bother me at all. I remember when Rochelle first got to our room, she asked me, "Moon, who do you eat with?" And Michelle answered for me because I paused slightly not knowing how to answer the question. Michelle replied, "No one... with whoever's standing next to her in line. I wondered the same thing: I was like who's that Moon's eating with and then realized she don't even know those people." I've realized more and more that image is everything in prison. I don't mind being a loner because I don't really ever go out to the yard or the dayroom. But I have noticed that I feel more uncomfortable when I go to chow because I am one of the only people who goes alone; and I feel like everyone else is aware of it too (it could also be that I'm one of the five Asians on this yard so I'm a bit more noticeable). I don't know why I even care. I just want my typewriter so I can chill in my room and write. I may never go out to the yard.

It's probably best to stay to myself and not get into the mix, as they say. That's how people get into trouble. When Lori first got to the main yards, she was on B yard and someone in her unit just got raped—they had the whole crime scene roped off and detectives coming in and everything. Apparently some girls locked one girl in a room/cell and sodomized her. I don't know what happened to the girl they sodomized or why they did that to her, but Lori got out of that yard asap. So far everyone I've encountered has been decent to me and I want to keep it that way; and the best way to do that is to keep to myself (because bitches in here are hella sensitive). I did stand up for myself this morning at breakfast, which I'm kind of proud of. This one woman was trying to collect juices to make pruno (i.e., homemade wine), so she was trading parts of her breakfast and noodles for juices. When she got to me she said, "Hey Chinese lady, you gonna drink your juice?" I looked her in the eye and said, "First of all, I'm not Chinese: I'm Korean. And I was planning to drink my juice." Then she half jokingly threatened, "Remember I work in the canteen." And I laughed it off saying, "That's fucked up." If she would have approached me differently, I might have traded her something for my juice; but now I was determined to keep it for myself. The pruno lady must have thought I was a punk because once she realized I wasn't giving up my juice, she turned to Adela and said, "Adela, get me that juice from her." Adela grabbed my juice for a split second but I gave her a very serious look so she immediately let go (plus Adela's one of my roomies so she's gotta respect me a little bit). Then I name-dropped a bit, which actually seemed to work. The pruno lady has a very distinguishing marking: a scar across her cheek that goes from her ear to the corner of her mouth (I don't know if you're familiar with that scar but that's a scar given to snitches: apparently, according to Sheila, Cubans gave this woman her scar). I remember Sheila (and Rochelle) mentioning this woman one time but I don't remember exactly what they said. I figured that Sheila was probably a big man on campus (she did four years straight at VSP and she sold drugs from marijuana to crack to heroin) so I thought it might boost my image slightly in the eyes of the pruno lady if she thought I was friends with Sheila: if she thought I wasn't some punk, F.O.B. newbie who doesn't know anybody. Well it seemed to have worked, but not in the way I expected. After she tried to get Adela to snatch my juice, I asked the pruno lady, "Hey, do you know Sheila J.?" She responded, "Yeah," but not in a happy way. After that she didn't badger me for my juice anymore. Hopefully her and Sheila aren't enemies to the point where I would get punished for dropping Sheila's name or being associated with Sheila, which is what I initially worried about when I first saw the pruno lady's reaction. I doubt it though—I think I'm just fine. I am glad I stood my ground though.

I'm sorry that this letter is so prison-centric; but the main purpose was to ask for your help regarding my quarterly package, so it just spun off from there. I miss you tremendously. I hope I get a letter soon. I love you and hope everything is going well in your life.

With Continued Love and Affection,
Jennifer ☾, R.P.L.

• • •

VSPW (Valley State Prison for Women), Chowchilla, CA

Tuesday, 11/18/08

My Dearest Jonathan — ♥

It's been so long since I've had any contact from you. I'm beginning to think you no longer exist. I hope you are well and that everything is good in your life. I miss you dearly and hope to hear from you soon. I love you my darling.

I met with a counselor yesterday; and I'm definitely endorsed here at VSPW, so I shall be here until I parole on 5/20/09. That part is fine because at least I can now get my quarterly package and special package(s) instead of possibly having to wait if I was eventually transpacking to CIW [...]. Now the thing I'm concerned with is the type of job I'm gonna get.

I want to be a teacher's aide, but the counselor I saw who is supposedly not my assigned counselor wants to give me a gate pass, which allows an inmate to leave the facility to work on the farm or the ranch or whatever they call it or the warehouse or the administration building. This stupid counselor (and I'm only calling him stupid because he called me a dummy after reading my confining offense) wants to put me to work in the orchard pruning trees. I told him I'd rather not and I have two degrees plus teaching experience so I think I'd be better put to use helping fellow inmates obtain their GED's. His response was, "This isn't Burger King: you can't have it your way," which he apparently thinks is exceedingly clever because he said it a few more times during our conversation, which later became a debate about Capitalism. Then I explained to him that I have a history of skin cancer and can't have prolonged sun exposure (which I learned I need to obtain a work chrono from the doctor to restrict me from working outside), plus I told him I'm not into robot-equivalent jobs (because I can also get a gate pass to work inside a warehouse or in administration as a porter, which is basically cleaning, or as a clerk but this dude is seemingly against me working as a clerk: he's really pushing the physical labor positions on me including kitchen, which I have worked food service before and I absolutely hate it). So after I briefly described what a robot-equivalent job is, the counselor dude went on describing, in detail, the finesse and complex decision making skills involved in pruning an orchard tree. I don't believe it though. I still think a robot can be programmed to do it because all the decision making he described is based on fixed circumstances or, at most, a combination of fixed circumstances or factors. I know you don't feel the same way as I do regarding robots liberating the workforce, so I once again want to reiterate that I am not putting a value judgment on robot-equivalent jobs. I am aware that they can provide meditative advantages or results for people and are necessary to maintain a society, especially a world society. I am simply stating a fact: the fact that most jobs the majority of the population are enslaved in can be done by robots/machines. And people can meditate on their own. Robot-equivalent jobs ultimately prevent people from being able to explore new life opportunities and discovering their true passion(s). I went off on a tangent so let me return to my meeting with the counselor.

After the counselor described the process of pruning trees, he (I forgot his name) ended by saying, "...and I can get you paid a little" (not all jobs are paying jobs: apparently there are less paying jobs than non-paying jobs). The counselor added that bit of information because he thought it would help me abandon my disdain for robot-equivalent jobs and jump at the opportunity for a bit of money. My response was simple and short, "Well I'm not a capitalist so that doesn't matter to me." And that spurred on an entire debate, which I was not entirely prepared for (it was notably odd when I began attempting to formulate ideas and then verbalizing them: it felt like I was speaking for the first time after just being awoken from a comma—or how I imagined it would feel since I've never been in a comma). I won't go into word for word detail describing our debate, but I do think it would be helpful for us (you and me) and the revolution to note his major concerns and misconceptions (seeing as how they most likely represent the concerns and misconceptions of the majority of the population unknowingly enslaved by and openly hailing the seeming "freedoms" of capitalism) so that they can be addressed in our manifesto (in which you have already produced a viable introduction to). Before I outline his defense of capitalism, which I will write out in bullet-point format, I think it's important to note that this particular counselor is a balding, straight, white male in his fifties, most likely, and is obviously conservative and who I later learned is an ex-C.O....

[...] I need to interrupt here for a second because my crazy cellies are drinking fucking hand sanitizer! Adela came into the cell clutching a plastic trash bag of clear liquid, all sneaky and suspicious looking. Once our door locked shut, she started acting more crazy and hyper than usual—she was definitely super excited and happy about something. Apparently she stole it from the cop shop, I assume. Isn't that friken rubbing alcohol in hand sanitizer?! Adela, in her instant drunken state, just begged me to try it. I had to basically scream at her, "No, it'll ruin my sobriety date!!", over and over again. (A few nights ago Adela offered me one of her anti-anxiety meds. I forgot the name of the medication but I assume it was some kind of benzo. I said no to that too, after asking her a ton of questions about the drug because for a few seconds I seriously contemplated taking it. There are many ways to get wasted in prison; but don't worry, I'm still seriously committed to my sobriety: the most I've done is buy and/or smoke less than ten super pinner-sized, hella expensive, and often stale tobacco rolled in tampon paper shared between at least three people.) Now Rachel is arguing with Adela, trying to get some more diluted hand sanitizer mixed with coolaid (I spelled it differently from the name brand Kool-Aid because it's not real Kool-Aid: it's some state, sugar-free drink mix that everyone calls coolaid, which I think is kind of weird that they call it that). Adela is refusing to give Rachel more drink. Adela's argument is "You don't bring nothing to the table. You have five fucking girlfriends and you have nothing to show for it. You need to tell one of those bitches to give us at least a noodle or something!" Everything here, it seems, is a hustle: nothing's for free. I paid $7.00 for two pairs of state-issued jeans because the pants they gave me were all huge (XL's). Granted the state jeans I bought they no longer make, like the baseball T's, so they're kind of a rare find and they were small, which is also rare; but to have to pay for state shit is kind of sad. Yet I suppose people survive off their hustle, especially if they're indigent. And women in here are scandalous. I hope lesbians on the street don't behave like this. But Rachel, for example, has a wife on the streets, a girlfriend on this yard, another girlfriend on B yard, and a girl in our room. Girls here are crazy players like that. And they are super insane possessive. If you have a girlfriend and definitely if you have a wife, you basically can't talk to anyone else. Rachel's public girlfriend is Christina. When Rachel's with Christina, Christina doesn't allow her to talk to anyone else; so Rachel behaves very standoffish and noticeably weird when friends approach her and she's with Christina. And then there's Adela and her girl, Erica. Erica's a 23 year-old lifer and they were together the last time Adela was in prison. But now they're not officially a couple because Erica doesn't want to be in a relationship (because apparently Adela hurt Erica by not being there for her when Adela paroled the last time—though Adela's madly in love with Erica). Yet even though they are not together, Erica will not allow Adela to be in a relationship with anyone else nor even allow Adela to be too chummy with anyone else. For example, Adela was sitting in the yard with this one girl. The girl was sitting close to Adela, playing with Adela's hair. Erica saw this and came up from behind Adela, wrapped her arm around Adela's neck and said, "Get up." Then looked hella hard at the poor girl and said, "Who are you?" Later that week, Erica jammed up Adela's friend in the bathroom and started grilling the poor girl, saying shit like, "Do you know who I am? How do you know Adela?..." whoop de woo woo (which is prison jargon for "blah blah blah" or "yadda yadda yadda"—sometimes they just say "woo woo woo"). After the bathroom incident, the poor girl came up to Adela and said, "I thought you and Erica weren't together... Sorry we can't hang out anymore 'cause I don't want any problems." And they aren't even a couple per Erica, which is the crazy part; so you can imagine how much more severe it could be when it comes to actual girlfriends or, worse, wives. And Snow was absolutely correct when she said I should not give relationship advice in prison. My advice always stems from expansive love ideals, but here in prison it is so intensely and wholly possessive love that girls cannot even comprehend what I'm trying to say—our paradigms of love are on the opposite sides of the spectrum. I don't think love even exists here: it's pure ownership. I am so glad that I am not ingrained in prison culture and existing from prison mentality like so many of the girls here because it's pretty horrible and sad, not to mention excruciatingly unexpansive. I hope to continuous expansion that I never have to come back here.

[...] I just had a serious breakdown: the first time I cried about my situation since I've been locked up. It's now Saturday, 11/22/08; and it seems once again I am not going to be able to call you. First of all, it was fog status this morning, which basically means we're (i.e., the entire facility is) locked down (i.e., confined to our cells) because they are afraid we might escape in the fog. Then unit C4 had some kind of incident (C4 is known as the trouble making unit): they had a code 2, which means an officer from each unit has to go to whatever unit has the code 2 and help out—which also means the entire C yard is locked down. So finally around 1 pm, they released C yard for main yard (we only get main yard, where all three yards [B, C, & D] get to go out to the main yard all together, on the weekends) and for noon meds only. They didn't say dayroom was open but I went out there anyways to try to use the phone because I've been waiting for this day for so long—two months—and I haven't received a letter from you in over three weeks! I am desperate to talk to you. So I was standing out in the dayroom in front of the cop shop hoping they were gonna let me sign-up to use the phone. This asshole C.O. was yelling, "The dayroom is not open; yard and meds only! Anyone still in the dayroom, I will take your I.D.!" Then he turned and looked directly at me; so I responded, "I can't go outside. I don't have shoes on" (I just had my chanclas on). He asked, "Why are you out here then?" I said, "I wanted to see if I can use the phone." He just looked at me like are you serious?! So I blurted out, "I don't know. I've never been here before." In which he responded, "Bullshit!" I was standing there dumbfounded, wondering what about me made him think this was not my first time in prison. I must have looked distressed because this girl called, Baby (by the way, Baby is a popular name in prison) who was across the street on A yard with me, came up to me and asked very sweetly, "What's wrong?" The asshole C.O. said, "Help her out. She looks confused." In which Baby responded, "She probably is. She's never been here before." The asshole shook his head and ordered, "Go stand by your door." I wanted to ask him when the dayroom would be open but he immediately barked, "What part of go stand by your door do you not understand!" On the way to my room, Baby explained that they're probably not going to open the dayroom; though they have no reason not to—they just don't want to. She said if they open it tonight, I can sign-up to use the phone tomorrow (Sunday). My heart immediately sunk and I had to hold back my tears while I waited for the asshole to open my door (and when he did, I paused to ask him if the dayroom will open anytime today; and he simply ordered me to get in my cell). I was so disappointed, distraught, and generally upset—feeling more alone than I ever have since being here—that I climbed on my bunk, crawled up in a ball facing the wall and sobbed silently to myself [...]. I haven't cried like that in a really long time. Crying where I can't hold back the tears. I didn't cry like that when I was taken away to jail after my sentencing. I did uncontrollably cry (because I really really did not want to be crying) when I was being booked into jail when I first got arrested for the attempted robbery though. But that was because I didn't think they were actually going to arrest me and I was terrified of kicking. And the other time I recall sobbing somewhat recently was when I received Colin's first mean letter. But that was based on feelings of guilt. When I cried today it was because I miss you so much. It's because I've had no contact from you in over three weeks and I can't help it but that does concern me a bit. I've been trying so hard to not let it bother me. I've been telling myself that you probably have been writing me but that the mailroom was backed up across the street, which is why I didn't get any mail the last week and a half I was there. And then I moved over here to VSP and any mail sent to Chowchilla now has to be rerouted, which takes a few weeks. And I've only been at VSP for a week and a half, which is probably not long enough for me to receive new mail addressed to VSP. But then again, this is all speculation and assumption because I also have to consider the possible fact that you haven't written me, that you no longer love me, that you are caught up with another girl, that we are no longer R.P.L.'s (maybe, hopefully still R.P.'s but no longer with the L). And now I'm gonna have to wait a whole entire week to maybe get the chance to call you again. I absolutely hate and am somewhat resentful of the fact that I can only call you on Saturday and that isn't even a guarantee that you'll answer. And it's so often that we're locked down that I may not even get to use the phone Saturday mornings or at most 'til the afternoon because I know you go to the musician's meeting in the evenings. Yet I know it's unreasonable to expect you to stay home waiting for the possibility of me to call; and I also don't want you to do that. I'm just feeling especially sad, frustrated, disappointed, and lonely for you right now. I just want some contact with you (even if it's just to tell me that we are no longer L's in our R.P.L. moniker). Fuck it, I'm just gonna try calling you whenever I get the chance to use the phone. Maybe you figured out a way to unblock your cell phone and put money on it so I can call you directly. And hopefully I'll get a letter from you this coming week. I do feel better writing all this to you. I apologize if it makes you feel uncomfortable or bad. That is not my intention. Plus all my fears are most likely manifestations of my own insecure and sad mind. I love you expansively, Jonathan; and I hope that whatever the case may be you are happy and healthy and always expanding/transcending. I miss you, my dear dear love... my heart aches for you and I love you...

It was so so nice to talk to you on the phone this morning. It was nice to hear your voice. And it was especially nice to hear you laugh and giggle in that exceedingly cute way of yours. I apologize again for starting off our conversation basically yelling at you. I couldn't take the disappointment of failing once again to connect with you on the phone. And I couldn't understand why you weren't picking up after my mom just called you to tell you I was gonna call right then. And previously I was reeling with horrible speculations of why you weren't home or why you didn't want to talk to me because you knew I was gonna call at that time, so I thought you were trying to avoid me or had an engagement more important than me (i.e., you were with your new love interest). And then I had the added stress of going over my fifteen minute time slot, worrying that at any minute the person who had the 8:15 am slot was gonna start yelling at me to get off (like what happened to the girl using the phone next to me). So it was this combination of sheer desperation, panic, fear, frustration, and annoyance that led me to yell at you at the beginning of our first phone conversation after two long months of not hearing your lovely, sexy voice. I am sure you were not expecting that sort of reaction from me; and I do sincerely apologize for that. And of course none of my fears were true. You were not trying to avoid me nor were you out with your new girlfriend: it was simply a misunderstanding of you thinking my mom meant 8 pm. And the reason it took four times of me psycho-dialing your number before you picked up was because your phone wasn't ringing due to low battery power. The only valid concern I had was going over my fifteen minutes of allotted phone time, which could have resulted in a battle because I was determined to talk to you. [...]

As I was planning on saying before my parenthetical indulgence, I was fortunate that no one was in desperate need to use the phone at 8:15 am because it allowed me to talk to you, which I am hugely grateful for. And I apologize also for my shameless display of insecurity, which resulted in me asking you six million times (or rather six, as you had said) if you and I are still R.P.L.'s, if you still love me, and if you have found someone else to replace me; and the variations of those three inquiries. I am fairly certain that you and I are uniquely connected, that we are meant to be, or at least our relationship deserves more than the less than two months we spent intimately together and the nine months of correspondence. Yet one can never be too certain when it comes to issues of the heart. Therefore, it helps and is necessary, I believe, to be continually reminded of one's position because feelings so often change. So I hope you understand and are sympathetic to my situation.

[...] Now let me go even further back in my letter (to page 3) and finish up my last uncompleted topic and provide the bullet points of the concerns and misconceptions expressed by creepy counselor/ex-C.O., Mr. Theissen.

- First of all, doofus-head doesn't even understand what capitalism is. He thinks all forms of bartering and trading (as in among the Indians, for example, before the colonization of America) is capitalism. Capitalism first developed in England as an idealized concept of a free market system as opposed to aristocracy (the development and definitions of capitalism are easily outlined in Capitalism for Beginners [...]). So it seems necessary that we define capitalism in the manifesto for all those ignorant of the system that not only oppresses them but informs their very desires and belief/value systems.

- This highly unaware moron also doesn't believe the majority of the population live in poverty or at least in the lower class (and this is throughout the world as well, largely due to American Imperialism). Therefore, we may need to provide statistics supporting this fact. Also, it is imperative to stress and explain that the very existence of capitalism is entirely dependent on the majority of the population being laborers: i.e., poor, maneuvering through life with a constant feeling of lack, always in want of something more. As long as capitalism exists, there will always exist a massive, majority of working class poor.

- One of the hugest misconceptions I hear over and over again is that if everyone's basic survival needs (i.e., food, clothing, shelter, health care) are provided for free, then everyone will become lazy. I think, in fact, I know, it will actually be the opposite. Without being enslaved in some robot-equivalent job in order to merely survive, people will have the opportunity, which is now considered a luxury, to explore and discover their true passion(s). People who love what they do work harder and better at it.

- Mr. ignorant-capitalist exclaimed that if he busts his ass farming, then he's not going to just share it with any lazy motherfucker looking for a handout. There are so many fucked up things in that statement, I need to break it down. First of all, he assumes that everyone is inherently lazy. And by the way he was talking, it seems he places a hierarchy on the various forms of work. It seemed obvious to me that he values hard, physical labor above all else because it means you're not lazy. I think probably many people believe this misconception. This is another reason (but certainly not the most important) why I believe in robots liberating the workforce. If robots take over all the hard, physical labor, people's concept and associations of laziness will change. Mr. limited-mind also doesn't see value in people who don't provide survival needs. For example, one person may provide inspiration to the masses, but he doesn't see that as an equal trade deserving of food from HIS farm because he's not getting anything physical/material or something personal to him in return. Mr. Theissen doesn't understand that the inspiration of the masses also inspires him, even though it is not directed to him specifically. Mr. Theissen requires something tangible or personal to be of any value. (By the way, Mr. Theissen also doesn't value the arts because he made a comment about not going to the movies because he doesn't like actors because they're overpaid. That may be the case, but so are athletes and he didn't say anything about them; and I'll make a bet he's a sports fan—once again valuing physical activities over creative ones.) And the hugest problem with the exclamation Mr. so-called-counselor made at the beginning of this bullet is that his thinking is entirely informed by concepts and ideals of ownership. He believes since he did all the farming, all the foods are his and he's not gonna share with just anybody. His personal feelings of self-worth are determined by things outside of himself: how much he labors and toils and the fruits of his labor are things he owns—his property and possessions—and his level of self-esteem is proportional to the quantity and quality of his labor and the fruits of his labor. So once again it comes down to issues of ownership and possessiveness.
- Mr. ultra-capitalist also believes that a socialist system is about

control. He said, "So you want to control how much food people get like in Communist China or Russia." Unfortunately I don't know enough about Communist China or Russia to respond to that. Perhaps you can. But I did say that communism has never been implemented correctly. It generally turns into a dictatorship so, therefore, it's more an issue of enamoration of power than communism or socialism. Secondly, I asked him why he must think of it in terms of control because I think of it in terms of providing—providing for people not controlling them. I explained to him that much of the revolution comes down to shifting the way people perceive things: from control to provide, from a culture of constant, unending wanting to that of desiring continuous expansion, from ownership and possessiveness to the elimination of all owners and possessive-type thinking, etc., etc.

Those are the main topics of debate I had with Mr. Theissen. Oh and also the capitalist concept of rugged individualism and "every man's an island." He doesn't quite grasp the fact that we are all connected, all of us including the multitude of various things in this world combine to form what I call the 3CE (3rd Communal Entity). He doesn't see how the continuous expansion of everyone and everything on this planet and beyond will benefit him. He is essentially a selfish, self-seeking motherfucker. We need to show these unknowing fools how the revolution will benefit them personally, which it ultimately will.

Wow, I'm finally done with this letter. I hope it wasn't too unorganized and all-over-the-place for you. And I also hope it wasn't too boring or repetitive or uninteresting. […] And I finally received your letter sent to Chowchilla written on 10/30 and 11/02. I got it last night, 15-20 days later. Thank you for writing me. I look forward to your second letter mailed to VSP (and hope to get more). I will respond to your rerouted letter in my next correspondence because this letter is already too long and I want to finally mail it off tonight and all my pencils are dull. I love you. I miss you. I'm glad you are alive and well (or getting better regarding the folliculitis). And I'm glad you still love me.

Always with expansive intentions,
Jennifer ☾, R.P.L.

• • •

Sunday, 11/30/08

Dear Jonathan,

I really hate saying this but I am incredibly mad and hurt right now. I think this is the first time I've been seriously mad at you. I'm mad and hurt at the same time because I don't understand why you wouldn't have the phone charged knowing that I was going to call you Saturday or Sunday morning and especially since this same exact thing happened last weekend. Maybe my mom was correct when she said, "Maybe he doesn't want to talk to you." Whether you're conscious of it or not, my mom is probably right and even though it hurts me to no end. Because if you really wanted to talk to me, you would make sure the fucking phone would be fucking charged. It's hard for me to believe that it is just a coincidence that your phone battery was low or dead two weekends in a row—during the only time out of the whole entire fucking week I can call you. And that's another thing: why can't I call any other time during the week?! I know you are super busy but you can't make a little time for me? I can't even express my anger and hurt to my roommates because I'm embarrassed to say that you only allotted time for me to call you on Saturday or Sunday at 8 am. I know what they would say, "Your man only lets you call him at 8 am on the weekends! And then he doesn't even have the phone charged! Oh no, he's got to go!" And I know it's not that important for you to talk to me either because in your letter where you gave me all those definitions of the word, worship (which I have an issue regarding something you said about that as well, which I will address after this), you wrote, "It's pretty unlikely that we'll connect though because I work on Sat. or Sun. every weekend and next two Saturday's I'll be out of the house jamming for part of the day." And then you throw in, "It would be great to talk to you though," which sounds so incredibly insincere. If you really wanted to talk to me, you would make it a little easier for me. Let me just tell you that early morning phone calls are hard to follow thru on this time of year. It's fog season right now and when there's fog, there is no movement, meaning we are all locked in our cells until the fog lifts (except for critical workers, and they have to be escorted to work by a C.O.). And when there's fog it is almost always in the early morning: the only time I can call you. This is what happened yesterday, Saturday. I signed up for the phone at 8:15 am but since we were on fog 1 status, I could not use the phone. I just got lucky today that there was no fog, but it didn't matter anyways because your phone was dead. Now I wish there was fog because then I would be ignorant to the fact that you don't care to talk to me. I just wish you would communicate this to me more clearly and directly, instead of making off-handed comments in a letter and making sure I can't get thru to you by continually having your phone battery dead. Please, if you no longer want to be with me, if you no longer love me, if you have found someone else, just please tell me so I can let you go. The sooner it is done, the easier it will be on and for both of us.

[…] But perhaps I am jumping to conclusions because I just told DC and his (or rather, her) girlfriend, Marshay, about today's phone fiasco and they didn't respond the way I said they would at the beginning of this letter (but then again, DC and I kind of have a special bond and he will always try to make me feel better). DC asked me what was wrong and I told him I was mad at my R.P.L. I explained to both DC and his girl, Marshay (because she was out of bounds in our room at the time), about what happened and about what my mom said about the possible fact that you may not want to talk to me. Marshay's immediate reply was, "Boy's are stupid that way. They always be doing dumb shit like that." She was referring to you not having the phone charged during the one time out of the entire week I can call you and especially after the same thing happened the week prior. But you know me, I don't like to categorize, stereotype, group people based on things like sex or gender. I don't believe boys do stupid things like that in general. Plus, I would like to think you, personally, are more aware and thoughtful than that. Yet, on the other hand, you are slightly on the self-absorbed side of the spectrum (which I will also address later and which I am also not placing any judgment on). So perhaps it was that you simply were not thinking of me or forgot that I was gonna call, which is also quite sad in itself too. And perhaps this is what Marshay was referring to when she said boys always do stupid shit like that, meaning they can be thoughtless.

So then I continued because I wanted more reassurance and asked, "So you don't think my mom is right and it's not because he doesn't want to talk to me?" Marshay responded, "Well you'd think that since you're in here if he didn't want to be with you, he'd just tell you. But then again, men lie all the time. And he might not have the balls to tell you," which I can see that as a possibility with you because, as you had admitted to me, your immediate inclination is to not break up with someone and, instead, indulge in a secret life. […] Yet, I hope it's as DC so sweetly said to reassure me, "Don't worry Moon. Your R.P.L. still want to be with you." So we shall see tonight because I got lucky and was able to sign-up for the phone again tonight at

8:15 pm. So if some other fiasco happens on your side to prevent me from talking to you once again, then I'll know something's up (because I know my mom called you to tell you I'm gonna call you tonight at 8:15 pm).

[…] But maybe you don't understand what it's like here, as my friend, Cindy, pointed out. For example, they just called fog 1 right now so my 8:15 pm phone call just got fucked off. (Not to mention the laundry fiasco that just happened. I had a laundry slot at 6:15 pm to 7:15 pm but they called fog 2, which means the yard is down but we can still do laundry and supposedly the dayroom and sometimes the phone if we're lucky. So once they called fog 2, everyone who had the last 7:15 pm laundry slot started freaking out because the fog was getting thicker and they were gonna call fog 1, which means no movement or complete lock down, at any minute. So my roomies, DC and Adela, were both yelling at me because I started a second small load of whites. And I'm jumping up and down and yelling back at them, throwing a small fit, because I still had 20 minutes left of my wash time; and I know neither of them would cut their wash time short for me [plus this is the first time I ever got to wash since I've been here]. And then my old bunkie, K-Luv, who's a lifer is yelling, pressuring, and criticizing this poor girl to get her clothes out before her time was up too. Saying shit like, "Hurry up! What are you doing?! Taking your clothes out one by one! I have never known anyone to take out their clothes one by one! What kind of stupid shit is that!" And then this other girl who lives across the hall from K-Luv started yelling at K-Luv because this other girl's clothes were being washed with the poor girl's. This other girl was arguing with K-Luv saying, "You don't run shit! Her slot is 'til 7:15 so if she wants to wash until 7:15, she has a right to fucking do that! You can't tell her what to do! You act like you run shit but you don't!" They were arguing so loud, the C.O.'s had to break it up. And when we came back to our room, Adela started really yelling at me about the laundry, blaming the fact she didn't get to finish washing her incredibly huge two loads of laundry on me, even though I had nothing to do with it because she wasn't even using the same machines as me: DC was after me, not Adela. So this is an example of how a simple thing like laundry, especially in combination with fog, can easily turn into a crazy drama causing incredible amounts of stress.) […]

[…] Okay, I need to stop here because I just received another rerouted letter you sent to Chowchilla (CCWF). Apparently you mailed two after the Norman Mailer article, not one. And this one I just read is so sweet and loving! Oh 3CE, I am the one now who feels bad! I am so sorry Jonathan. Please don't be too upset or angry with me for freaking out on you. […]

[…] The absolute best part of your letter was at the end when you wrote, "And yes, I'll definitely come pick you up when you get out, no matter where you are." Oh Jonathan! Thank you! I love you!! I didn't want to mention anything about that because I figured if you didn't respond to my request for you to pick me up, then you must not want to. So I wasn't gonna bring it up again. Oh but how you just made my day, my week, and possibly even my entire stay in prison! You are so good to me and I most definitely feel loved. Thank you for loving me. […]

So I have other things I wanted to tell you about that's been going on with me here in prison. And I also want to respond to your three letters. But I'm gonna write another letter to put in front of this letter to warn you of my incredibly huge freak out displayed throughout this long letter; and I'll include all that in my preface letter. I love you.

With sincere and deep apologies for my displaced anger and frustration,

Jennifer ☾, R.P.L.

• • •

VSPW (Valley State Prison for Women), Chowchilla, CA

Tuesday, 12/02/08

My Dear, Sweet, Loving Jonathan — ♥

I hope my letter you received just prior to this one wasn't too upsetting for you. I actually thought it wasn't that horrible (after reading it over a second time). I do get a little dramatic though, indulging in self-pity and the tragic, romantic heartache of a potential lost love. And you have vocalized on more than one occasion a concern that I may think too highly of you, that I am blind to your faults. So I hope my last letter helps you to see that I do not put you on a pedestal, that I have no problem telling you things that may bother me about you. It is simply that I am one who doesn't easily get bothered by people. Yet let me tell you, I was hella mad that Sunday morning when your phone was dead. […] I apologize for lashing out on you. I was already highly stressed that particular Sunday morning because I came so incredibly close to loosing my sobriety the night before.

So I think I mentioned this before but only on the weekends during the daytime do they let all three yards (B, C & D) out at the same time to program together on the main yard (they used to in the evenings too until somewhat recently when this one girl got jumped and killed; so now they only let one yard out at a time each night, alternating yards every night). So a lot of activity and exchanges occur during the weekends because it's the only time out of the week (other than maybe at work) when you can meet up with people from another yard. So needless to say, a lot of people get high on the weekends and they also re-up on their supply if they are selling drugs. DC often comes back hella stoned (smoking weed), for example. That one particular Saturday (this one that just past), both Adela and Rachel came back high from snorting H [*heroin*]. At first it didn't bother me because they were complaining about it being bunk, especially Rachel (but she's only done it four times). Adela complained a little bit but she was also talking it up with me because she knows I'm a dope fiend (and so is she). As soon as Adela came into the room, she exclaimed, "Moon, guess what I just did?" And again, like I said, I truly did not care at first. But then I started noticing their behavior. They might have complained they weren't high, but they sure as hell were scratching a whole lot and even nodding slightly at times and I could see it in their faces. So then I started asking Adela a lot of questions, like confirming the cost of one skeet or paper (that's what they call it in here because it's basically a smear of H on a piece of paper) and if she could tell me how much in weight or equivalent on the streets a skeet/paper is. I would ask her one question and then I would be like no, no, never mind, I don't care, I don't need to know that. A few minutes would pass and I would ask, "Okay, can you SHOW me how much it is?" because she couldn't give me a weight and she claimed it was $10 worth on the street but the way everyone was describing it, it seemed significantly less than that. And then again I would be like no, no, I don't want it. I went back and forth like this literally like five to seven times. Even Adela commented on it, laughing she said, "Listen to Moon. She is such a dope fiend! She can't help but want it even though she's trying to tell herself she doesn't." That's when DC told me he had one if I wanted it but that he won't give it to me now; he'll ask me again tomorrow so I can think about it and make sure I really want it. I told him firmly no, don't ask me, I don't want it. Then I proceeded to try to get my mind off of it by playing a mindless game of solitaire, which of course did not work. I sat on my bunk, flipping the cards with increasing frantic, rising pressure and frustration as I rationalized and justified me using just once. After about five minutes, I came to the conclusion that I'm in prison so I deserve to get high just once. And I even decided that it wouldn't count because I'm in prison: as if I'm in a dream world that isn't real, that whatever happens in prison doesn't count, like I just discovered a loophole in sobriety. I wasn't going to tell you or anybody because it was only gonna be this one time and that's it (plus I decided it wasn't gonna count anyways): I was gonna continue maintaining my sobriety date of 3/19/08 (because for some reason my time is important to me so I had to rationalize a way for me to use and also keep my length of sobriety). I don't know if this happens to you, but once I allow myself to decide to use, it's all over, I'm off and running. The only times I haven't used when this has happened was when it was simply impossible for me to get any drugs; and fortunately this was one of those times. So after I convinced myself that I can use just this one time, I said to DC, "Okay, give it to me. I want it now." DC responded, "Naw cuz, I decided I don't want to be the reason for your relapse." And then I just snapped and started literally begging and nearly crying and yelling at DC, demanding that he give it to me now. Finally he said, "I don't even have it on me right now. I'll give it to you tomorrow." I didn't believe him so I started screaming, "I don't want it tomorrow! I want it now! I know you have it, DC! Just give it to me! Just fucking give it to me!!" Oh my 3CE, Jonathan, you should have heard me: it was an embarrassing display of desperation. So finally DC convinced me that he didn't have it by explaining that he never keeps shit like that on him in case we ever get searched, etc., etc. I was hella mad at that point because by then I really really wanted to get high, and I was thoroughly convinced I was going to. But thank continuous expansion I didn't or couldn't because my obsession passed and I am so so glad that I am still sober. It's just super scary how I have been so incredibly dedicated and completely into my sobriety for the past 8 months and how quickly and instantly I can let it all go. So needless to say, I was really stressed and disappointed in myself and scared and worried that I would freak out like that again in the future because I know my roomies are gonna get high again; so I believe that added stress intensified my freak out on you regarding your phone being dead. But don't worry, I'm back on track again—I no longer want to get high.

After my freak out on DC in my room, Twin (who is super-Christian yet very sweet and also into her sobriety) came up to my bunk to talk to me. She explained how it's not worth it because she had a bunkie who spent $30,000 trying to get high, trying to achieve a good nod, which she did maybe twice, Twin said. That's a hell of a lot of money to spend on drugs and not really get high. Because a skeet/paper costs $50 and though Adela claims it's $10 worth on the streets, Twin (and also Sheila from across the street) says it's more like $2 worth because apparently it's literally a smear, which if you were to ball it up, Twin said it would maybe be the size of one grain of dehydrated rice. Twin also warned me that though she loves Adela and thinks she's great, it will ultimately help Adela if I end up using, which is why Adela is pushing me to use. Twin said it doesn't mean Adela's a bad person (which I also agree with), it's just that this is part of Adela's hustle: it's the way she supports herself and makes money in prison and also gets drugs herself. I understand that and I also understand the nature of drug addiction and of the big H. I don't want to get caught up in all that horrible shit again and especially here in prison where I can run up a huge debt and get hurt or get caught using and have to stay here longer. I truly love being sober and I don't want to give it up for anything! [. . .]

I hope I didn't freak you out too much with the story I just relayed to you. I want you to know what's going on with me and also why I possibly over-reacted regarding the phone issue and incident. I mean, I'm bound to get tempted to use throughout my sobriety; so this was just the first serious one and, therefore, had significant effect on me. Thank continuous expansion for time-space continuum (i.e., the passing of time and movement thru space because feelings/obsessions eventually pass and fade if I can be patient and wait for time to pass; and feelings/desires/thoughts also change with my changing environments as I travel thru space, which this part is more difficult to achieve here in prison). But I am getting out of my cell more because the other thing I wanted to tell you is that I started working the day before Thanksgiving (by the way, how was your Thanksgiving: did you have a good meal, did you gather with people, etc., etc.?).

So of course the motherfuckers put me to work in the fucking kitchen, the one place I absolutely did not want to work (I'd much prefer the orchard over the kitchen). I think I told you this before but I worked food service my freshman and sophomore years at UCLA and I absolutely hate it; so my dislike of my new prison job is not purely reactionary and uninformed. I hate smelling like food mixed with cleaning solutions. And it would be a little easier to deal with if Ms. Anaya, the C.O. who searched our room that one Sunday when I actually talked to you on the phone (remember I told you our room was being searched because two of my roomies walked behind the C.O. when she was opening our door), didn't take most of my clothing: leaving me with only one pair of pants (other than the ones I was wearing), no shorts, and two shirts. She said I had excessive state clothing, which I did, though not crazy-style like most people here (I had two extra pairs of pants because like a sucker I paid Adela for state-issued pants that fit because it's so hard to get small clothes; and I had an extra pair of shorts). I am allowed to have three pairs of pants, four shirts, one sweatshirt, and one pair of shorts, oh and one nightgown. But Ms. Anaya only left me with (including the clothes I have on) two pairs of pants, three shirts, and no shorts (I had my sweatshirt on and she didn't take my nightgown). This may not sound like a big deal but one of the two pairs of pants has a hole right in the crack of the ass and the other pair is massive, I can barely keep them up (of course she took the small pairs that I paid for). And since she wrote on the confiscation sheet that I had excessive clothing, laundry won't give me another pair of pants or another shirt or shorts so that I can have the correct amount of state clothing. I explained this to Ms. Anaya and she eventually agreed to give me some of my confiscated clothes back. This is exactly what she said, "I'm working a double shift so I'll be here until 10:00 [pm]. Why don't you come see me after dinner or between 2 and 4 [pm]." So at 3 pm they had an unlock and I went out to find her but another C.O. said she's S&E tonight, which means she's working somewhere on the facility yard at the chow line or med line, etc. The C.O. told me she's working the chow line and to talk to her then. When I saw her and explained to her that I came out at 3 pm, this bitch fucking said, "I told you to see me before 2 [pm]." I couldn't believe it because I know what she fucking said; but you can't argue or debate or even question what they say—they can never be wrong or possibly make a mistake. So she's either crazy or has no short-term memory or she's fucking with me. But whatever the case it doesn't matter because all three possibilities lead to the same result: I got screwed. Ms. Anaya's response was a shrug and "You don't need shorts anyways, it's winter." Bitch, I don't care about the fuckin' shorts: I need pants! (I don't usually call women bitches: it's more of a joke because everyone calls everyone bitch here.)

Now this may not seem like a big deal to you and it really isn't that catastrophic to me either. It's just inconvenient and slightly uncomfortable; and you never know what can happen. For example, today (Wednesday, 12/03/08) is our yard's laundry day where we can turn in dirty, state laundry and get clean, different ones (we also have laundry machines in each unit so if we get good state clothes that we like, they suggest we keep them and wash them ourselves along with our personal clothes). So today is one of my day's off (my day's off use to be Sunday and Monday but that was a pay slot—I just happened into that slot because it was the one open at the time—but my boss told me on my first day that he was gonna give the pay slot to someone who's been there longer, which is fine with me: I don't need the money and it's only 8¢ an hour or $12.00 a month—isn't it ridiculous how little prisoners get paid). My new days off are Tuesday and Wednesday, which just got changed last night (Tuesday night, so I worked Tuesday). So as I was saying, I am fortunate that now one of my days off is also our laundry day. So I decided to turn in the pants that I wear to work to try and get a smaller size (we turn our laundry in at breakfast and we get them back by the end of the day). And I was pleased about this because when I use to work on Wednesday, I was never gonna be able to turn my one pair of pants in to try and get a smaller size (they are 2XL!) and even though my other pair of pants has a fairly big hole in the ass, they are small so there's no way I'll willingly part with them (because for some reason, it's exceedingly difficult to get small state clothes, which I would think would be easy because everyone wears their clothes oversized, baggy, and hanging below their ass). But like I said, you never know what can happen here. So of course they called institutional lock down because two scalpels are missing from the infirmary. So that means everyone must be locked down (except for critical workers, like me, who work in the kitchen because we need our food), which means our laundry won't get done, which means no work pants for me tomorrow, which means I have to wear my only other pants with the hole in the ass to work where they'll get all dirty and smelly, and I'll have to come home and be forced to wear my dirty ass pants all around and all the time because they're the only fucking pair of pants I have now. And we may be on institutional lock down for a few days or longer because apparently they are going to search every single cell in every unit on every yard for those damn scalpels, which are probably long gone by now, buried deep in the ground somewhere on the yard. That's gonna take a million years to search every single cell. They're doing B yard now (A yard is Receiving, which is separated by a wall—hence the term, "going over the wall"—so they probably skipped A yard). I really hate getting our room searched because they just throw our shit around, mess everything up, step on it, take shit, throw all our saved state food away, etc., etc. And we're all gonna get stripped searched too. Adela already shoved a small bottle of ink (for tattoos) up her ass. And they're stripping out every critical worker going to and from work, so I'm gonna get stripped going to work tomorrow, which sucks because I'm on my period; and when you get stripped, they make you take out your tampon or pad so you have to stand there naked for like 10 minutes with blood dripping out your vagina and down your leg. Isn't that a nice visual for ya?

It's now the next day, Thursday (12/04/08), around 10:30 am (I don't go to work until noon: my hours are 12 pm to 7:30 pm). I want to apologize for complaining so much. Honestly, it really isn't that bad here. I think because there is so minimal stimulation here in prison that little, stupid shit like not having enough pants really starts to bother me. And even here in prison, things always seem to work out. Because yesterday, before we were locked down, Adela raided the confiscated clothes and this morning she gave me two pairs of small pants (and she didn't charge me this time: I think she charged me the first time because I was new and she wanted to see what she could get out of me). And we got our laundry back this morning too; but the motherfuckers didn't give me back a pair of pants even though I turned a pair in. See this is what I mean when I say you can never know what will happen (especially when it comes to laundry). So if Adela didn't give me those two pairs of pants this morning, then I'd be really screwed because laundry fucked me by taking my only other pair of pants. Now, thanks to Adela, I have exactly the right amount (3 pairs), which is good because Mel, the C.O., just told us to put all our excess clothing out in a bag because they're getting ready to search our unit. Laundry also fucked me out of a shirt (they gave me a nightgown in place of the shirt I turned in), so that's my next mission or actually Adela's next mission (she's good at getting clothes).

I'm sorry I'm writing about really inane things. As I just said, prison is really not that horrible. But I think a lot has to do with if you have a good room or not because 80% of your time is spent locked in your cell with all your roomies. So if you have one of those fascist-type rooms with a reigning dictator watching and criticizing your every move, then your time is gonna be significantly more difficult to bear. The more I talk to some of the girls here, the more I appreciate and am exceedingly grateful for my room. I now know that my room is a rare exception: it is unique and uncommon. Even though some of my roomies may get high occasionally, at least none of them are strung out or selling drugs out of our room. And every single one of my roommates is cool and hella chill and relaxed. None of them even really gets moody, which is surprising especially during the times when we're all locked down together for 24 hours and longer. I absolutely love my room and all my roomies! I hope I never get moved and no one moves out. Most of the time, we just laugh and laugh and laugh. Twice I made DC laugh so hard he literally cried—tears were streaming down his face. It truly feels like summer camp most of the time, not prison; but that's only because my room is so fun and my roomies (especially DC, Adela, and Rachel) are so friken, hella hilarious. And they all love me.

Adela one night was talking about how important it is to see someone's paperwork (pap smear results, hep C & HIV test results) before engaging in any sexual activity. Then she said, jokingly in her fake Russian accent she does, "Otherwise we'd all be in here fucking each other." And then Adela looked at DC and said, "We'd all be in here fucking Moon!" Don't worry though because I only want to have sex with you. I have absolutely no desire to have sex with any of these bitches. I think they think I'm more endearing than anything anyways.

I just got home from work and I am fucking tired! I am not use to manual labor or I'm hella out of shape. I don't really work in the kitchen around food: I'm a dock worker, which means I load up all the food in a truck and deliver the foods to A/B kitchen and C/D kitchen. It's actually quite a workout because the food containers can be heavy and hard to push and pull (a lot of upper body strength, which I don't have). The other half of the job is primarily cleaning: washing or rather hosing down the food containers we use to transport the foods as well as the quick chill racks, sweeping and moping the entire kitchen, cleaning the inmate and staff bathrooms, emptying all the trash, etc., etc. I worked fuckin' hard today and I am damn tired. And after we were done with the kitchen tonight, the sergeant made us dump all the confiscated stuff from B yard (remember I said they were doing room searches throughout the entire prison; and they're still not done with B yard). It was sad because they confiscated a lot of stuff: we threw away CD players, headphones, personal photos, and seemingly endless bags and bags full of shit. I would be hella mad if they threw away my pictures of you. I think that's kind of mean and unnecessary.

Anyways my love, I am so tired. I can't think straight. And I want to see if the C.O. will take this letter when s/he comes by for room check around 10 pm because it's Thursday so if this letter doesn't get in the mailbox tonight, it won't go out until Monday. I love you. I miss you. You are always in my thoughts. I will write you another letter to respond to the three letters I received from you (two you sent to CCWF and the first one you sent to VSPW).

I hope to dream of you tonight in my sleep:
I, who am so very much in love with you
and also currently suffering from exhaustion,
Your Revolution Partner/Lover,
Jennifer ☾, R.P.L.

P.S. I just reread/proof-read my letter and noticed I said "hella" a lot. I don't ever say that when I talk. I mostly say that in my letter(s) to you as a joke. I have not yet adapted my speech to that of prison dialect. Oh and I wasn't able to get this letter out last night, so unfortunately it won't leave the prison until Monday. Love you!

• • •

VSPW (Valley State Prison for Women), Chowchilla, CA

Tuesday, 12/09/08

Dearest Jonathan — ♥

I received your handwritten letter you wrote on the back of the New Yorker article about child rearing. I got it on Friday, 12/05/08. Thank you. I have yet to finish reading the article because work makes me so tired that I just come home and veg out watching DC's TV; and I've also started to nap after breakfast from 7 am-10 am. Then I go to work from 12 pm-7:30 pm, slaving away performing the epitome of robot-equivalent jobs; and then I come home and start the horribly unexpansive cycle all over again. I fuckin' hate my job, Jonathan; and it just got significantly more unbearable because I yelled and literally cried at my asshole boss, Robles (not my super cool boss, Bravo). I called him a fascist. I said he was enamored with power and desires to oppress his workers (the people he depends on) because he's a miserable person who just wants to make everyone around him miserable. I yelled, "You work fucking food service! You're not a C.O.! But obviously you want to be!" I actually started this rant with Robles the day before yesterday (on Sunday) and it continued and came to a head last night. And I'm embarrassed to say it was over a ducat to pick-up my special purchase (my CD player). My super cool boss, Bravo, told me that as long as I have a ducat, he'll let me go get my box(es). But unfortunately, Bravo goes home at 2:30-2:45 pm and box ducats during the weekdays are in the evenings. When I asked Robles the same question, he said no. And I snapped. I really truly go mad. That's when I called him a fascist and all that. And that was on Sunday. So of course that evening I got a ducat to pick-up my CD player the next day, Monday at 5 pm. I don't have the energy to go into detail about this but it ended Monday night with me jumping up and down screaming at Robles about love and compassion and revolution. And then Robles ripped up my ducat into tiny little pieces, which made me burst into tears (because now I wouldn't even get to go after work to pick-up my box, with no ducat). This may sound like a really stupid thing for me to cry about, and I admit that I over-reacted a bit and threw a slight tantrum. I think, perhaps, I cried more out of frustration and hurt feelings that I couldn't convince Robles to care about the well-being and happiness of his workers, inmates, and other people in general. Robles is fine with and feels justified at being oppressive and a fascist asshole. He and C.O. Wells were laughing about it (and at me) while I was crying and screaming, "I will not let you break me! I will not allow you to change me into someone like you! Even though you're an asshole and oppressive and a fascist and mean to me, I will always perceive you with love and compassion because that's what I believe in!"

It's embarrassing to me that I got so incredibly and unusually upset about not being able to get my special purchase because it's a material item and I pride myself in not being tied to material objects and possessions. However, being locked up, simple things like music and a typewriter and good shampoo and thermal underwear become exceedingly important. Boxes (i.e., quarterly packages and special purchases) are one of the very few things we get to look forward to. It is true, according to the CDC rule book, that unless we have a yellow, priority ducat, regular white ducats do not have to be honored by our boss or C.O. But why the fuck wouldn't Robles honor an R&R ducat knowing how important they are to us? And I can tell you for certain that there would not have been slack in work for the less than one hour I would have been gone (he has plenty of workers and a lot of time half of them just sit around or socialize). Not to mention that I work hard (which has been noted by one of the C.O.'s and the Culinary Sergeant), and I worked extra hard that day. The other thing that really bothered me was that I was told by a few of my co-workers that Robles has let people go get their boxes while at work before. And on that day, two of my co-workers asked Robles about it and he told them he was gonna let me go. So I feel like he was fucking with me: getting my hopes up throughout the day only to continually smash me down. And the other thing is that I've been told during orientation that R&R will only ducat inmates three times for packages and after the third time, if we don't pick it up, they'll send the package back. And I can't help it: I really really want my boxes.

Before my full-on tantrum with Robles, I had a debate about this issue with the Culinary Sergeant, Sgt. Heffington, and the C.O. on duty, C.O.

Wells. I won't go into horribly boring detail about it; but at least with these two, they were willing to engage in an actual discussion or debate with me where we present our opinions and back them up with facts or personal experiences, etc. Robles, on the other hand, would not even give me that respect. And I'm sorry to say this but it could also be that Robles is simply incapable of debating (i.e., he is simply not that intelligent—he probably doesn't even know what a fascist is). The incredibly sad part about my debate with the Sergeant and the C.O. is that it confirmed my belief that the majority of C.O.'s view us inmates as less than, as not worthy of love, compassion, and respect. As they said, "Most of you don't want help. All you guys want to do is hang out on the yard and homosect and act like thugs. If I was loving and compassionate to all the inmates, then I would walk around with shoe prints all over my back." (By the way, homosecting means engaging in homosexual activity: I have never heard that word before, I think it may be a CDC-invented word.) I completely disagree with them. In my experiences, if I treat people with sincere love and compassion, I generally get that in return. And my cool boss, Bravo, is a perfect example of that. Because Bravo is cool and nice and respectful, all his workers love him and would happily do anything he asks. None of them take advantage of him nor view him as a punk, like the C.O. and sergeant argued. The C.O. and sergeant said that I am naive and don't know what I'm talking about. "Come back and talk to me after you've been here for three years," they said. The thing is I am aware of how prison culture is—I just operate from a different, nearly opposite, framework than they do. [...] It basically comes down to the fact that most C.O.'s are repressed themselves—they have internal fascism—so they know no other way to be. Even though C.O. Wells and Sgt. Heffington alluded to the fact that they have tried the loving and compassionate way, I seriously doubt they have because they simply don't know how and don't believe in it. But the absolute worst and most disturbing and depressing part of this entire scene and issue that I created was how my fellow inmates and co-workers reacted toward Robles after my fit.

When I discussed this issue with all my co-workers, they all agreed with me: we were all on the same side because they want to be able to get their boxes too. I felt like I got them all rallied up and that they understood about revolution and how we need to all band together in support of one another if we ever hope to make a change. Yet once they got in front of Robles, all they did was basically kiss his ass. When I was jumping up and down, yelling and crying at Robles, they were all laughing at me, which didn't bother me that much because even I could see the humor and ridiculousness of my behavior (even when I was in it). But what did really bother me was afterwards, when I had calmed down and went to ask Robles and C.O. Wells their names and titles so that I could write a 602 against Robles. During that time, C.O. Wells and I engaged in another minimal, low-key debate. A few of my co-workers were in the office at the time cleaning up. And while I was debating with C.O. Wells, the girls were snickering, rolling their eyes, and exchanging knowing glances at Robles. Finally PB (short for PlayBoy) said, "Enough already. I don't want to hear this shit anymore," which then made me mad at PB. The thing is, PB only really cares about herself. She wants to get her box so she thinks siding with Robles and kissing his ass will help her get it. And the other girls, even though they agreed with me when I was talking to them alone, once they were around Robles, it was all smiles and giggles. How are we ever gonna achieve a successful revolution if, when it comes down to it, people only care about themselves and what they can personally get and how they can personally benefit? [...]

[...] Earlier this week, I had a bonding moment with all my roommates. I believe I mentioned to you that I decided not to shave while I'm here in prison, and that includes my pubic hairs. When my roomies noticed I didn't shave my legs, they inquired about it and wanted to see my hairy underarms and also my pubic hairs. That was one of the times I made DC laugh so hard he literally cried. They were all screaming and laughing about it and we all had a lot of fun, including me. When they saw my pubic hair, Adela was like you gotta shave that shit. And I was like no way. I explained that when I'm on the streets I trim it but in here fuck it, there's no need. But later on, especially when I was on my period, I realized that perhaps there is a need for me to tidy up that area a bit because my hairs were getting exceedingly long. Now, as I am with everyone, I am extremely open with my roomies. I talk at length and in detail about my bowel movements, the discharge from my gynee, and the dried menstrual blood on my pubic hairs. When I was discussing the latter with my room, Adela exclaimed that this is why I need to shave it off. I finally agreed with her but explained that I don't know how to shave my pubic hairs. And Rachel immediately jumped up and volunteered to do it for me. This caused a bit of conflict because Lori is Rachel's bitch in the room only (because Rachel's a bit of a ho and already has a public girlfriend on the yard and also a wife on the streets); so Lori didn't want Rachel to do it. Lori said she would do it instead, but Rachel insisted that she should be the one to do it because it was her idea; and everyone in the room was on Rachel's side. I said I didn't care who did it, so I decided it should be a room effort where it will be performed out in the open and everyone could be involved. So this past weekend (I believe it was Saturday evening), after I was completely done with my period, my roomies propped me up on the table and completely shaved off all my pubic hairs. It was loads of fun. Adela laughed so hard she fell over on top of my bunkie, Diane. Rachel was so funny because she seemed scared of my pubic hairs at first. And DC and Adela were telling Rachel what to do. And Rachel was getting defensive saying, "I know how to do it!" Yet Rachel seemed scared to touch my gynee area. Finally Adela yelled, "Just grab the turkey and pull it to the side!" Adela was referring to my labia because, as you know, I kind of have big labia. [...]

Since we're on the subject of my gynee, do you think my labia are unusually large? I use to be super self-conscious of my labia but I'm not so much anymore. I hope you don't mind them. You would tell me, right? After my shaving, I asked Adela and DC if my labia are abnormal (because I'm sure both of them have seen numerous pussies). Adela said, "They are big, but I'm more shocked at how tiny your pussy is! I have never seen a pussy as small as yours. Your R.P.L. must bang the shit out of you!" And DC kept repeating, "He does fuck the shit out of you, haw Moon? Does he? He does, I can tell." [...]

If you noticed on the envelope, I have moved to B yard. This just happened last night (Wednesday, 12/10/08). I so desperately did not want to move because I loved my room so much; but unfortunately they ended up giving me a gate pass, so I was forced to move to B yard. At least I don't work in the kitchen anymore with that fascist fuck, Robles. Though I may have endured that job only to stay in C3, room 28. I'm currently in B3, room 15, which is in B hall; but I will only stay in this room for a few days because I now work in "greens" and all "greens" are housed in C hall (we are called "greens" because we wear light green prison outfits). The room I'm in now seems fine so far but I'm gonna move, so there's no reason for me to get too comfortable. I hope hope hope that my permanent room will be non-oppressive. But I seriously doubt I will ever get a room as great as my room on C yard. I loved all my roomies and I feel a great loss right now—I feel really alone. DC was so sweet. He kept saying, "Oh Moon, I don't want you to go." And then he would periodically look at me and say, "Oh Moon-head, eyes, nose." It was cute the way he said it. He's the baby of the room.

I have yet to start my new job. I just got my new job ducat Tuesday night. But I couldn't work yesterday because I can't go to a gate pass job from C yard—I need to be on B yard. And today we've been on fog 1 and 2; and since I'm no longer a critical worker, they haven't called me into work, which is fine with me. It says on my work ducat that my new job is "Warehouse Shipping &" (which I assume is shipping & receiving). I work from 8 am to 4 pm, Monday thru Friday (Saturday and Sundays are my days off). I'll tell you more about it once I start working.

I'm gonna end this letter here. I will write you again (and respond to your letters) once I move to my permanent room in a few days. So maybe hold off writing me until you get my next letter with my final housing location because sometimes it takes a week or longer to re-route mail even if it's only down another hall in the same unit. I hope I haven't been too critical with you in my past few letters to the point where you now find it difficult to deal with me on whatever level. I love you, my sweet, loving Jonathan: you are absolutely the best thing in my life.

Thinking of You Always,
Jennifer ☾, R.P.L.

• • •

VSPW (Valley State Prison for Women), Chowchilla, CA

Friday, 12/12/08

My Dearest Love — ♥

I don't much like the room I'm in right now; though it's really not that bad. I haven't moved to C hall yet but I'm hoping I will by the time I mail this letter (on Monday). I just don't feel comfortable here, but I suppose that's normal whenever one enters a new environment, especially a new living arrangement. Like right now, it's probably around 9 am and we're on lock down because of fog (and also because they're doing flu shots), which means no programming (i.e., no school or work), so everyone's home and asleep (except for me and Misty, the most oppressive one in the room or as Blunt called her, "The Wicked Witch of the West"). Misty, just this morning after breakfast, asked me and my bunkie (who also just moved into this room the same night I did) if we could please not slam our lockers shut because it scares her and she has a bullet in her chest, etc., etc. Now I hardly ever even close my locker all the way, unless I'm gonna lock it, because it is loud at times. But I didn't say anything about it. I was just like yeah no problem. I've learned, just in the two days of being in this room, that contradicting Misty will only lead to misery. Yesterday, Misty yelled at her bunkie because her bunkie's sheet accidentally fell a little off her bunkie's bed and hit Misty. Misty's bunkie (I can't remember her name) was arguing that it was an accident. Misty's rebuttal was that it may have been an accident but she has to be more careful and aware of other people, she needs to be more considerate of the fact she has someone living below her. Now Misty has a valid point (though I think she's a little extreme with it, getting upset over a friken sheet touching her), and her point would have more validity if Misty herself would abide by her own argument of consideration of others. Because just a few moments ago, Misty was making noticeable noise, shuffling thru her locker, and woke up her bunkie. Her bunkie said something about it and Misty got defensive saying, "I'm not being that loud and you can't expect it to be silent in here." It's funny (or rather, sad) how the ones who are the most fascist, claiming oppression/repression in the name of consideration of others, are seemingly the most inconsiderate and hypocritical and unaware of their own behavior. Because, also yesterday, Misty argued with Diamond as well. Misty was yelling and then crying how she doesn't understand why people won't leave her alone because she just keeps to herself and never tells anyone what to do or gets in anyone's business, woo woo woo. And I was sitting there thinking, are you for real because I just met you and I've already heard you complain and tell three people what they should be doing and how they should be doing it. I sincerely cannot understand how people can be so hyper-aware and hyper -critical of other people's behaviors and seemingly, completely ignorant of their own (especially when they're talking about the same behavior!)—it truly blows my mind.

And this is a perfect example of how oppression/repression only just breeds more O&R [*oppression & repression*]. Because Misty likes to harp on stupid shit like the sheet accidentally hitting her, people (like Misty's bunkie) get resentful and reactionary and similarly start harping on equally stupid shit like Misty shuffling around in her locker. So now this room has a stifling O&R air about it where I am currently afraid to even move. I'm serious about this, Jonathan. Everyone's asleep and it's dead quiet in here. For some reason, my bed makes loud creaking sounds whenever I shift positions, so I'm scared to move. I also needed something out of my drawer, which is under my bunk, but the drawers make loud sounds when you open and close them. I tried to open my drawer slowly and quietly but

I got scared by the noise it was making so I just left it half open. And I'm hungry and I want to eat my cookies but the plastic wrapper makes a lot of noise, so I've been waiting for people to flush the toilet to get pieces of my cookie out. Isn't that sad? And I literally walk on my tiptoes so my sandals don't make noise. My other room was not like this at all. The whole month I was there, there was not one argument. No one complained about or criticized other people's behavior. And if someone wanted to sleep during the day, they would wear earplugs or just not mind the noise of everyday life. Many people here confuse consideration and respect of others with O&R. Because everyone in my other room was definitely considerate and respectful of everyone else in that room—they just did not participate in O&R.

I'm sorry if I sound like I'm complaining a lot. It's more of an observation. I think I just miss my room and all my roomies, and no other room will ever compare to that one. I just hope my more permanent room isn't worse than this one, because it can be a hell of a lot worse. This woman, who also just recently moved into this room, came from a room where she wasn't allowed to watch her roommate's TV when it was on—she couldn't even look at it! Now that's crazy. 3CE, please don't put me in a fascist room. I guess we shall both see by the end of this letter.

Since I'm on the topic of O&R, I also recently had an experience where I blatantly perceived someone who was successfully convinced to desire her own repression. When I moved to my current room, I happened to move into the same hall as one of my ex-co-workers: her name is Taz. When we saw each other, Taz brought up my incident with Robles. Again, I will not bore you with all the details: I will just relay the parts which support my opening sentence. So at one point, I was explaining to Taz (as I did to you in my last letter) the perceivable difference (and results) between how Bravo interacts with and runs his crew and how Robles does. [...]

[...] I used Bravo as an example of how someone in a position of power does not need to be an oppressive fascist in order to get respect and results from his/her workers. In fact, I believe the opposite. Yet when I brought up this example to Taz, she responded, "Bravo's only been working here for a few months. He doesn't know any better. Robles has been here for years, so he knows. Once Bravo's been here for a while and inmates start taking advantage of him, then he'll change. They need to be that way in order to get respect. If they were loving and compassionate, then inmates would run all over them," etc., etc., or woo woo woo, as they say here. When Taz was saying all this to me, I was looking at her in awe, in total shock, because she was nearly reciting, word for word, what C.O.

Wells and Sgt. Heffington said to me. And I was equally shocked because Taz is the most vocal fan of Bravo. Just a week ago, Taz went on a rant in front of us and Bravo about how she checked a girl for talking shit about Bravo. Taz said, "People can talk shit about Robles or Johnson or whatever asshole boss in the kitchen, but not Bravo. Bravo's cool as fuck and ain't no one gonna talk shit about my Bravo in front of me." Yet now, Taz has been brainwashed to believe she needs to be O&R'ed in order to be good or behave or not take advantage of people or however you want to put it: in one week, she has been made to desire her own repression. I tried to explain to her that there is a difference between being nice and loving and compassionate and then being a push-over or a punk: those two modes of being are not mutually inclusive. Taz was beginning to understand and agree with me, but unfortunately, our conversation got cut short. (By the way, apparently my little tantrum got around the kitchen staff because just right now at dinner, Johnson came up to me and told me he heard about my tantrum and then asked me what exactly is a fascist. I must have explained it better to Johnson because he was agreeing with me, especially when I said Robles should treat his workers, the very people he depends on, with kindness and compassion and respect.)

Wow, my current temporary room is kind of crazy. Since I've been here, Misty and Diamond have been arguing non-stop. And tonight after dinner, Diamond and BA got in a full-blown fist fight (I just sat on my bunk and ate my piece of cake, which I smuggled out of the chow hall, and tried not to look). And now Diamond's in the bathroom cutting herself. So there's all this drama surrounding that amongst all Diamond's play sisters, brothers, aunties, cousins, etc. in the room (which this whole play, pretend family structure that exists in prison is another subject I will discuss after this). Now everyone's yelling at Diamond because apparently we can all end up in the hole or get "life in prison," as they keep saying, if Diamond ends up dead while we're all in the cell. And before that everyone—except me, of course—was downing the pruno or hooch or baby they were laying in the room, trying to get rid of it, because the C.O.'s were doing room searches because someone stole phenobarbitals from the nurse's station. And everyone smokes cigarettes non-stop in the room. It is true what they say, all the tobacco is on B yard because all the tobacco comes from people who have gate passes, like me now. I even broke down today and bought three cigarettes for almost $7 (or one can of roast beef, a bag of rice, a pack of AA batteries, and four noodles). I couldn't stand watching and smelling all the smoking and not having any for myself. I'm even considering muling or packing it in when I start working greens—not to sell it but so I can have a supply for myself—because it's way too expensive to buy. But then again, maybe not because knowing me I'll get caught and lose my date and have to stay here longer. And Misty is hella particular about how things should be in the room and how someone should clean, etc. This morning after breakfast (it's now Sunday, 12/14/08), Misty lectured us new people that we cannot walk away from the sink, even for just a few seconds to get a towel, before spraying it down with disinfectant and wiping it clean. And yesterday morning, Blunt made a comment about being really annoyed and looked right at my bed because I didn't have time to make it before going to breakfast. For some reason that really irked me; and I thought to myself, "If only these motherfuckers cared as much about the fact that more than half of their fellow inmates don't have a high school education nor have any awareness of who they are or what their true passions are or about the fact they are so severely repressed to the point where they only care about really stupid, inane things like how one should place her shoes under her bed." Fuckin' prison: I'm beginning to hate it here and I hope I never ever come back. I'm sorry I'm talking so much about prison culture. It's just that I've become more inundated in it—having to witness it right in front of my face—since moving into this room. I just want to mention one more striking detail or structure that exists within prison culture: the family unit (and then I'll stop, I promise).

So inmates who are immersed in prison culture or want to be—usually the youngsters—get adopted by an elder, usually a lifer or long-timer; and the elder becomes their play mom or play dad (if the elder is a stud-broad). And from that, a family unit is created with extended family: sisters, brothers, cousins, aunts, uncles, etc. And my current, crazy, high-drama room is just brimming with this ridiculous unexpansive family structure. BA and Blunt are brothers because they have the same dad (all three are studs, obviously). Rosie and Diamond are sisters because they have the same mom. Misty is Diamond's aunt because Diamond's mom is Misty's niece. And Rosie and Blunt are cousins thru some relation. And they rarely call each other by their actual names. Instead they say, "Hey brother" or "cousin," "sister," and of course "mom" and "dad." In my other, bestest, most unoppressive room ever, DC had a mom and an auntie; but it wasn't all crazy-style like it is here (DC was the only one in our room who was involved in this pretend, play family; and DC wasn't all crazy-style into it like they are here)... Oh my 3CE, Diamond and BA just got into another fight and this time, BA was chocking Diamond and socking her in her face so Diamond scratched the fuck out of BA's face (apparently Diamond and BA used to be a couple—this is a prime example of why C.O.'s warn inmates not to get a girlfriend in prison). Jonathan, there is way too much drama in this room. I can't wait to get out of here. But it's true what they say, as long as I stay to myself and mind my own business and not get into the mix, I'll be left alone. During this last fight and thru all the yelling and screaming, I sat on my bunk quietly writing my letter to you and acted like nothing unusual was going on—I didn't even look in their direction. I was so quiet and unnoticeable, huddled on my bunk in the corner, that Misty forgot I was in the room. Misty commented about it, saying, "I forgot you were even in the room." She was slightly concerned because she was saying things she didn't want random people to know, like the fact she has dope on her. I just told Misty, "I'm not even listening," which seemed to satisfy her. Fuck Jonathan, I just bought three more cigarettes. I'm gonna end up trading all my canteen for smokes at the rate I'm going. Oh, I just learned that Blunt and Diamond are brother and sister because they have the same mom but not the same dad, which is why BA and Diamond are not siblings (or maybe they are but they just don't call each other brother and sister because they were fucking). I don't know, it's actually kind of confusing. But in any case, the whole thing is telling of how unexpansive prison culture is because you and I both know that the traditional family unit is one of the most O&R base structures in existence, besides Judeo-Christian beliefs and values. Because, just how the family behaves out in the free world, it is magnified here in prison. Not in terms of, perhaps, molestation or physical/ emotional abuse, but rather, in terms of the hierarchical power structure and siding with and protecting blood over all others. I wish there was a way for me to get my fellow prisoners to desire continuous expansion over O&R or, at least, desire revolution over non-conformity for the sake of non-conformity (which, in here, is actually conformity or the convict, bad-ass mentality). Definitely if I was gonna be here for a long time, that would be my primary mission. But since I'm basically just passing through, I'll just observe and take note: research for the future, for the revolution—another experience to help me relate to and understand a significant, influential, and seemingly growing sub-culture.

[...] It's Saturday afternoon (12/20/08: yesterday was my 9 months of sobriety). I spoke to you on the phone this morning; and you wanna know the funny, yet intensely infuriating, thing that happened right after I got off the phone with you? Remember how I said on the phone that my current room's not that bad anymore, that it's cool now and I feel fairly comfortable and that even Misty and I can joke around. And remember also how I had to take a shit. Well, fucking Misty and I got into a huge fight, which almost resulted in my very first fist fight, because I took a shit while she was in the middle of cleaning. Now it is common knowledge that when Misty cleans, she wants all of us to stay out of her way and sit on our bunks, which I have no problem with. However, there have been two times before today when I've had to take a shit while Misty's cleaning; and I've asked her permission and she bitches and moans but it's never been a huge problem (and other people in my room have done the same thing). So this morning when I came back into my room after getting off the phone with you, Misty and Diamond were cleaning, so I asked Diamond if I can use the bathroom. Diamond then asked Misty if it was okay and Misty, in her usual grumpy demeanor, said, "Go ahead." I'm in the bathroom putting the toilet seat down and I'm using a piece of toilet paper to do so and here comes Misty thru the bathroom window yelling, "I just cleaned the toilet! It's sterile! You don't need to do all that! Just sit your ass down!" Now I have this habit (and I'm aware that it may fall into the category of OCD) of laying down toilet paper on the toilet seat before I sit on the toilet (and I do this on my own toilet in my own house and I've been doing this for years so it has nothing to do with my roomies or how I view them in terms of cleanliness). Misty noticed me doing that one day (as well as some other of my OCD-like tweaks that I do) and has been giving me grief ever since. Her argument is that people might take offense to that, which it is obvious that she takes offense to it because she's the only one out of all the rooms I've been in to say something about it. Misty's offended that I line the toilet seat with toilet paper, yet she freaks if one of us walks away from the sink without spraying it with disinfect and wiping it dry after we brush our teeth. Misty constantly yells about communicable diseases yet she's offended that I want to lay toilet paper down before I sit on a toilet that eight women share. I don't fucking get it. So anyways,... I just spoke to you on the phone and told you all about this incident, so I won't repeat myself. Misty and I are cool now, but I'm still looking forward to moving rooms because I'll be moving into a green room; and everyone who works greens is short-term with low points and, therefore, less likely to be oppressive and controlling.

[...] I just want to say one more thing about my battle with Misty and then I'll finally respond to your letters. The main problem I see with Misty and other established prisoners is actually an AA thing: people here are overly concerned with what other people are doing—taking their inventory, as they say in the program. And whether Misty is willing to admit it or not, it all comes down to control, no matter how seemingly veiled it may be. For example, last night, after both Misty and I had calmed down, we were able to have a mature, adult conversation about our high-emotion dispute of the morning. We were talking about me moving to a green room and Misty said that I'm gonna miss this room because a lot of greens don't clean so the rooms are dirty. And I said I don't care about that as long as the room isn't oppressive. And Misty's response was that being in a dirty room is oppressive. I strongly disagree because, first of all, I doubt the rooms are as dirty as she claims. And second, if it is dirty, I'll simply clean it. What I think is oppressive is when prisoners are repressed to the point where they force their notions of cleanliness on others. No one in my other magnificent room ever told anyone to clean or how to clean and that room was spotless. I have always thought that this country's obsession with cleanliness is a direct result of O&R and of capitalism (i.e., creating a demand for more products, such as anti-bacterial soaps, hand-sanitizers, disinfectant wipes, various odor eliminators, singe-use disposable floor mops that only create more waste, etc., etc.). I told Misty that what these long-timers, lifers, and parental figures should be concerned with is building self-esteem and discovering personal, expansive passions of the youngsters they take under their wings to ensure that they never return to this hellhole, instead of badgering them about how they need to sweep immediately after brushing their hair or the manner in which they need to pour the water out of the plastic container to rinse down the shower walls. I have to give Misty some credit though because she did bust out with a good analogy. She used the example of the movie, The Karate Kid. If you recall (or come to think of it, you may not because it could have been before your time; but it's a pretty famous movie with long-term, residual references, so hopefully you do know about it), the Karate Kid's sensei made him perform a series of cleaning tasks, like waxing a car. Do you remember "wax on, wax off"? At first the Karate Kid thought these chores were stupid and didn't understand how they related to his martial arts training. But it turned out that the movements he used to put the wax on the car with one hand and then take the wax off with the other hand were the same movements he needed to learn in karate. So Misty's argument is that teaching the youngsters how to clean is the first step to building self-esteem as well as structure and discipline. And I am well aware of this school of thinking because it is also the school of thought subscribed to by most rehabs. I don't know how many times I've been forced to double scrub while some tech looms over me claiming that this will keep me sober. But the unfortunate fact is that, based on statistics, the relapse rate of addicts is still significantly higher than those who remain sober; and similarly, the recidivism rate of those who've been to prison is higher than those fortunate few who manage to never return. So the basis of my argument is that this school of thought obviously does not work. I'm not saying that everyone should be slobs and live in filth—I simply believe that the focus needs to be shifted from robot-equivalent-based activities and disciplines, such as proper, prison-based cleaning habits and excessive or non-functional cleaning (like raking invisible or non-existent leaves at Impact) to that which promotes, what I call, awareness-freedom and continuous expansion. Like with every faction we are attempting to implement within the revolution, it comes down to a shift in paradigms, rather than focusing on the multitude of various symptoms or effects or inevitable results of the reigning paradigm(s) currently in place.

It's Monday (12/22/08) afternoon and it doesn't look like I'm going to work today. We've been on institutional lock-down since last night because apparently they found a bullet in A yard, maybe in ad-seg visiting? Who knows really what's up, and I actually don't really care all that much anyways. All I know is that we're locked down and plus there was fog this morning, so I didn't have to go to work. I finally got my ducats to pick-up both my quarterly package and my special purchase last night. And of course, today, all this stupid, lock-down shit is happening so I may not be able to get it yet again. And then they'll have to re-ducat me, which will take another week or longer and woo woo woo. My ducat's not 'til 5 pm though, so I'm really really hoping that they'll find what they're looking for or finish with their searches by then so that they'll take us off lock-down and I can go on my R&R ducats. But even if they do take us off lock-down, I'm still at the mercy of whatever C.O.'s on duty at the time. And some of the C.O.'s are straight assholes or maybe they're just lazy or whatever the case: if they don't feel like releasing us for non-priority ducats, especially R&R ducats (because they don't view those as important, even though R&R ducats are probably the most important to us prisoners; or maybe the C.O.'s know how important they are to us, which is why they fuck us by not always honoring them), then too bad for us—I simply won't get my box(es) that day because the C.O. didn't feel like dealing with it. Let us hope that this will not be the case today.

So I think that I'm just gonna mail this letter off today and, once again, hold off on responding to your letters until my next correspondence. Hopefully by then (or by tonight), I'll have my typewriter and I'll be able to bust out letters faster, easier, and with more enjoyment. Oh and I'll also finally have music to listen to! And that will also help with all my various writing endeavors. I was so excited last night that I had difficulty falling asleep (like when I was a child, full of excitement and unable to settle down and fall asleep, knowing that I was going to Disneyland the next day). But I must not get too excited in case my hopes are crushed yet again by some authority figure enamored with her/his own power. Isn't it sad how we are encouraged to not have hope (and this applies also to the free world).

Well my dear, darling love: it was so nice to have talked to you twice this past weekend. I love you and miss you and count the days until we can share life, love, and revolution hand-in-hand and side-by-side. Until then my love...

Thinking of You Always,
Jennifer ☾, R.P.L.

• • •

VSPW (Valley State Prison for Women), Chowchilla, CA

December 24, 2008

My dearest love,

Obviously I finally got my quarterly package and special purchase packages. I am so fucking psyched. I absolutely love my typewriter! And what a difference music makes. I can't tell you how much more happier I am to be able to listen to music and good music at that. Life is so much more pleasant now. I guess it's true what they say, music is certainly good for the soul. [. . .]

[. . .] Living with eight women in a room too small for eight people can be so annoying at times. I knew my typewriter was going to be an issue in this room. When I started typing this letter, Misty came over to my area to discuss the noise factor. This time Misty was actually nice about it. She suggested that I maybe set up a time each day to type that is considerate of all the people in the room because, as the example Misty used, people like to watch TV. I guess the typewriter is loud enough to drown out the sound of the TV. I don't know, I have my headphones on. The thing that kills me is there's no "program" set up for the TV: it seems to always be on (by the way, "programming" in prison can mean a number of things: I've come to learn that it basically means an allotted time to do something, whether it's work, school, yard, dayroom, and also apparently typing too). I suppose the TV is more ambient than a typewriter. [...] It's cool for me to type now though because everyone's up and being unusually loud. Misty, of course, just had to say something to me about it: she periodically needs to reassert her alpha status in the room. [...]

[...] I think our room may get searched again because everyone's freakin' out and moving shit around. Apparently they lay a lot of babies in this room and this room has been hit a lot because of that. Just yesterday Rod, a C.O., searched this room and took both BA's and Misty's babies that they were brewing for Christmas. Okay, I found out from Rosie right now that they're searching the room across the hall so they're worried they may be searching the entire hall. I don't really care because I don't have any contraband. The only shitty part is that if they find something in a common area in our room, like for example BA's baby was under his bed instead of in his locker, then they usually write everyone in the room a 115, which usually results in a loss of 30-90 days. I don't think that will happen this time though because either BA or Diamond will take the blame so all of us won't get a 115.

Okay, it's now Christmas day. Merry Christmas by the way. I don't know if you noticed but I'm not much into holidays. It's not because I'm locked up and depressed about being in here during the holidays that I fail to mention it. To me it's just another day. And of course Christmas is the epitome of capitalism: it has become the ultimate vehicle to promote consumerism and want. But since it is Christmas, my roomies are having people over to celebrate and be festive by drinking hooch (they managed to dig their babies out of the trash last night after dinner; and the C.O.'s didn't end up searching our room). I didn't feel like being around a bunch of drunk people so I grabbed my typewriter and my CD player and moved out into the dayroom. I actually kind of like it out here. I don't have to worry about making noise and I can also sing along with my music too (just not too loud). The only shitty thing is that there's no table, only benches, so I have to straddle the bench with the typewriter in front of me on the bench so I'm forced to stoop down. I'm sure this is not good for my posture or my back. I guess I should stop talking about inane, mundane things and get to my original agenda, which is responding to your letters.

So I finally finished reading that <u>New Yorker</u> article, "The Child Trap: the rise of overparenting." One of the best parts of that article besides the moral or selfishness issue of caring only for one's own children, is the statement, "Schooled in obedience to authority, they will be poor custodians of democracy." This is also definitely in line with the failure of the prison system: it seems obvious that gross amounts of authority only breeds more repression, which is I suppose what they want. Repressed people are easier to control. As Joan Acocella quotes Marano, the editor-at-large at Psychology Today, "'It may be that robbing children of a positive sense of the future is the worst form of violence that parents can do to them.'" I guess a determining difference is that we, us prisoners are no longer children: we are perhaps deemed a lost cause.

Marano stresses "over all others" how the trends of overparenting have always followed "insecurity bred of the global economy." That seems to make perfect sense like how Acocella adds, "No Child Left Behind: that sounds like the expression of a democratic wish. More likely, it was the product of an economic wish—that America not be left behind by India and China." I don't know, though, about Marano's statement of how the "robotic behavior" of the children "schooled in obedience to authority" will threaten "'American leadership in the global marketplace.'" You know I thoroughly do not endorse robot-equivalent jobs for humans; yet for a different reason. I don't give a fuck about the global economy nor the leadership role of America. I only care about continuous expansion; and robot-equivalent jobs, behaviors, and lifestyles simply are not conducive to expansion. I actually think that America and capitalism would want to produce more robotic humans because they make better laborers. And isn't it exceedingly sad about the 1998 study at UCLA? How the reasons for going to college degraded from the 60's ideals of "'becoming an educated person'" or "'developing a philosophy of life'" to the 90's version of "'making a lot of money.'" It seems at the root of everything is the issue of money and the economy: absolutely everything. This entire existence's obsession with money and the economy does nothing but degrade and devalue the world and all the people in it because as Acocella writes at the end of her article, "the percentage of poor children in America is greater today than it was thirty years ago."

I can go on and on about the various issues raised in this article but I don't want to bore you with reiterations of notions you are already familiar with, seeing as how these revolutionary topics are usually the primary subjects of most of our discourse. I do want to comment on one last thing in the article and then I'll move on. Carl Honore, along with some other writers on overparenting, are disgusted with the "self-esteem movement." He uses the example of "'every doodle ends up on the fridge door.'" Acocella continues with, "A review of thousands of studies found that high self-esteem in children did not boost grades or career prospects, or even resistance to adult alcoholism." This study may be true but I think it has more to do with the capitalist notion of high self-esteem: determining or gauging one's self-esteem by things outside of oneself such as, a doodle that ends up on the fridge. I strongly believe in developing an expansive-based self-esteem (i.e., loving oneself for the mere fact that one exists and not on who one is or what one does—a Michael influenced idea) as the basis for overcoming the multitude and often veiled forms of oppression and repression. To completely dismiss the emphasis on developing healthy self-esteem in children (especially in disgust) is wholly reactionary. As usual, the approach is not to abandon the notion entirely but rather to completely change the definition of self-esteem, for example; or better yet, the entire paradigm in which the notion supports. I enjoyed the article though. And of course, the most important fact that Acocella presents is how incredibly selfish parents are to not care for the lives of children who are not their own. She writes, "Hovering...is largely the preserve of upper-middle-class parents..." This may be true when it comes to hovering or overparenting, specifically; but the emphasis on one's own blood family—the caring and support of one's blood over all others—is prevalent throughout all economic classes. It could also even be argued that this unexpansive notion is even more pronounced in the low and poverty level classes because, as I've heard many times, "family is all I've got."

[...] Misty just told me that I've been typing all day, which I have, so she thinks it's time for me to kick back and watch a movie (which is funny because my bunk or bed is the only one in the room that cannot see the TV). But that's okay because I want to get this letter out tomorrow morning on my way to work. It was so nice to have the day off today. My job seriously hinders my work on the revolution. I wish I didn't have to work, but no such luck now that I'm greens, especially now that I'm going to be the procurement clerk: greens override everything (i.e., SAP, VOC, all jobs inside the prison, and the CALM class, which is only 2 hours each day and the rest of the time you can do whatever). I already mentioned this to you on the phone, but I am amazed at how quickly time passes in prison. And apparently it's not just me: everyone I talk to, even those who have been here for a few years, say that their time went by fast. Before I realize, it's already Friday: like now. You would think that it would be just the opposite: that time must move exceedingly slow for all the people locked up (I did). I have theories on why time moves fast here but I don't have the time or luxury to do so. I need to get off the typewriter. I love you an amount so enormous it cannot be quantified and in a manner so expansive, formless, and constantly transcending that it cannot be accurately described in words.

I miss you, my darling love,
Jennifer Moon, R.P.L.

• • •

VSPW (Valley State Prison for Women), Chowchilla, CA

December 27, 2008

Dear Jonathan,

Wow, I just got off the phone with you. That was definitely something I was not expecting. I'm still in shock. I have so much I can say; yet it is all so futile because nothing I can say will change how you feel. Once again, my dewy-eyed idealism and naive romanticism has gotten me into trouble, the kind of trouble where I am alone and heartbroken. But don't worry, my dear, it will not break me. I will always love you and think fondly of you and the short time we had together. I only hope the formlessness of our relationship will continue to morph, expand, and transcend to maintain our revolution-based partnership. Because revolution is all I have (and my art)—it is all I've ever really had. And as I've mentioned to you before, at least I get to be right about the fact that love will always be a tragic romance and forever elude me. I've always secretly thought (at first revered and then feared) that I will spend my life alone: meaning with no significant other, no lover. Yet I've always took comfort in the fact that I love life and this world and all the people in it. I will be everyone's significant other and lover (in a sense, not literally). Please excuse my indulgence in highly romantic notions of tragic love and the G&R-ing of my newly solitary status. I hope you understand because it's all I have, it's my saving grace, it's the one thing I know I will always have and that will never abandon me (not that you have), it's the thing that I'm leaning on, grasping, embracing desperately so that I don't fall to pieces in the anguish of a love lost. Plus, I'm listening to Nico, which is only helping me to indulge in romanticizing tragedy. Nico sings in Jackson Browne's song, "These Days":

I had a lover

I don't think I risk another these days
These days
And if I seem to be afraid to live the life
that I've made in song
It's just that I've been loosing
so long

I definitely will not risk another lover for quite some time, maybe never. I have been loosing that plight for so long. I don't think it's meant for me. I think I'm meant to save the world from oppression and repression. I know I'm reverting back to my delusions of grandeur; but again, it's the only thing that gives me hope and takes the pain away (even if only for brief moments). And it's better than using drugs.

This heartache feels different for me than others I've experienced in the past. Perhaps it's because I still doubt it: as my usual pattern, I don't believe you. A part of me still thinks that once I get out and we hang out, working on the revolution or music or art or whatever, that you'll realize that you still are in love with me or you'll fall in love with me all over again. But that's five months from now; and as of now, you claim to no longer be in love with me and I have to accept that no matter how much I want to deny it or rationalize it away. But I still believe, as you once also reiterated, that you will never find anyone who will ever come close to being like me (your words) or who will ever compare to me (my words). And I still believe, as you wrote so seemingly long ago, that I am the best you've ever known. Thank you for saying those kind things to me even though they don't apply anymore (because at least at one point they did).

As I said at the beginning of the last paragraph, my heartache over you seems unique and noticeably different than others I've experienced. Perhaps I've matured or have a healthier self-esteem or have expanded past co-dependency but I'm not completely devastated to the point of non-functioning capacity like I've experienced in the past. Or perhaps it's because I'm locked up, living in close quarters with a bunch of other people (a majority of them unsympathetic or at least uninterested in indulging in more tragedy) that I simply do not have the luxury to break down completely. Also, I don't view our relationship ending. It has simply changed to that of only R.P.'s. I have faith and trust you that we will still maintain an intimate relationship, just not a romantic one (romantically revolutionary perhaps :), not physically romantic).

Yet on the other hand, when I stop typing or intellectualizing and conceptualizing the fact we are no longer lovers, the pain I feel is so great that I truly feel like dying. My love for you is so complete that I now feel completely empty. I find myself wondering in desperation how I can so completely believe in our love, in our union, in our partnership, in our deep connection, while you are on the other end feeling nothing like that at all. Am I that blind, unaware, and senseless? I try to always be empathic, especially with you. I am a fool: once again fooled by notions and desire for love and for a partner to share life and passions. I know now that I am a fool, but I truly did believe we were going to share a life together. Our values, beliefs, artistic endeavors, sexual aberrations/fantasies, etc. were so in-line with one another that I truly felt we were meant for each other. Oh how can I forget our similar revolutionary goals. I want to scream at you to come to your senses: how can you not see we are meant to be R.P.L.'s!!? But again, I need to trust you: I need to accept the fact that you know your needs, desires, and emotions better than I ever will. So now I'm left wondering what I did wrong. I regret writing you that angry letter and being too critical of you at times. As Conor Oberst sings in the Bright Eyes song, "An Attempt to Tip the Scales":

> I think you lost what you loved
> in that mess of details.
> They seemed so important at the time.
> But now you can't even recall
> any of the names, faces, or lines.

As I requested during our phone call, can you please tell me what about me made you fall out of love with me (because you insist that it's not because I'm not around or locked up). If it's not situational, then it must be intrinsic. And you agreed with me over the phone, so please tell what about me made you come to the conclusion that you are no longer in love with me. I am at a complete loss. The only thing I can think of is the fact that I am now considered a convict or soon to be ex-convict. You have alluded to this concern a few times in letters, phone calls, and in person. Please understand that this is not who I am. I made a serious mistake, a mistake I'm already being punished for; so please do not punish me further. As Nico sings in the same Jackson Browne song:

> Please don't confront me with my failures
> I had not forgotten them

Committing crimes and engaging in illegal activities is not something I desire. I believe in continuous expansion; and a criminal lifestyle only closes down one's options rather than opening up more options. Fuck Jonathan, you already know this about me. I'm just typing to avoid shedding tears because whenever I stop typing to take a bathroom break, for example, I am overcome with intense sadness and horrible, devastating pain that I cannot describe. Please forgive my ramblings and my desperate attempts to understand the ending to the lover component of our R.P.L. relationship. Will we truly still remain R.P.'s? Is that what you really want or are you simply being nice and not taking everything away all at once? But if you truly believe in revolution, I do not see why you would abandon our partnership regarding that specific endeavor. Revolution comes first and we can only help each other. I don't know what I'm writing anymore. I am so sad and heartbroken: I'm afraid to cease typing. I hate being here. I wish I was out there with you. Then we could discuss all this in a more thorough and intimate manner. But what would be the point? It seems you've made up your mind. I hate everything right now. No I don't. I'm just uncontrollably sad. Everything seems surreal: the fact that I'm in prison, the fact that you just told me that you are no longer in love with me, the fact that I'm sitting on a bunk bed in a prison cell typing this pathetic letter to you... I feel like I'm in a horrible dream, a nightmare.

Please do tell me the reasons why you realized you are no longer in love with me because I think I at least deserve that. If we are to continue being R.P.'s, intimate friends, then we need to maintain the openness and honesty. I hope you agree, but if you don't please tell me.

You once told me that maintaining a friendship with ex-lovers is not always desirable nor practical for you. Do you feel that way about us? I am hoping our relationship is different and unique in that it is able to be formless and ever-changing, yet always intimate. Is this too much for me to ask for? Do you desire anything remotely similar to that?

I had better end this letter before I embarrass myself further with my pathetic attempts to keep you in my life. I suppose as everyone says, if it's meant to be, it will be. So please excuse my dewy-eyed idealism and naive romanticism, but I still think we are destined to be R.P.L.'s. I'm allowed to believe that.

Always with love and respect,
Jennifer Moon, R.P.

• • •

VSPW (Valley State Prison for Women), Chowchilla, CA

December 28, 2008

Dear Jonathan,

Thank you for accepting my call this morning and being willing to discuss your loss of love for me further. I definitely feel better now because the not knowing and the speculating was killing me. I also feel better because the reasons you provided are... how can I put this... well, wholly informed by and most definitely existing within the confines of the current power structures and paradigms, which results in repressed notions of being and desires. I feel like a love-sick fool for trying to convince you over the phone that we are meant to be R.P.L.'s and not just R.P.'s. If you remember, in my desperate state, I myself fell into repressed desires: I was crying trying to convince you that I can hold down a job and am able to produce a monetary income. Foolish ramblings of a fool blinded by love! If that is what you truly desire from me, then we are truly not meant to be. I am an artist and a revolutionary. I have absolutely no desire to waste my life away in a job that only helps to perpetuate capitalism or whatever O&R system. […] And since we're on this subject, my dear, what are your plans? You are going to music school in hopes to eventually become a successful musician or producer. […] So seeing as you are a musician desiring to work in the music industry, a realm equally difficult or even more so to break into as the art world, how can you possibly judge or criticize or question my intensions [*sic*]?

I suppose the difference is that you are more practical than me: I am too fantasy-based, not rooted in reality, as is your concern. You have a valid point with this one. I am painfully aware that this aspect of me is both part of my charm as well as my downfall. On one hand, my ability to think outside of current, over-arching, and often O&R paradigms, allows me to be a vehicle for change, expansion, new ideas or combinations, and the avant-garde. Yet, on the other side of the spectrum, I sometimes suffer from delusions of grandeur and have difficulty with follow-thru, which the latter only became an issue once I entered grad school. […] So I know this is something I need to work on. But don't we all—including you—have various issues or character defects, as they say in the program, that we need to work on. If you want to deem me an unfit partner or lover for you because of this one aspect of my current being (which, as I just explained, is both beneficial and potentially detrimental to my expansion) and ignore all the numerous great and expansive things I offer you as a partner/lover [...] then I must say, it is your loss (mine too, but at least I didn't initiate the ending and I attempted to keep our partnership alive). I know this may sound typical of any girlfriend being dumped, but I do sincerely believe you will not find anyone who will ever love you like I do, with complete willingness to understand and compassion and thoughtfulness and flexibility and sincere honesty. No one who will ever fully satisfy your sexual fantasies like I do. And no one who will ever inspire you to continually expand and transcend like I do.

[...] I don't know what your idea of a healthy relationship is but all relationships, whether intimate or functional (like a business relationship), is based on or eventually results in some form of dependency. You seem to be taking on a very straight, white male ideal of "every man's an island." You seem to strive to not be dependent on anyone and for no one to be dependent on you: you want the seeming strength of independence and desire to avoid the burden of seeming responsibility for another. You care too much about maintaining a "pure essence" of yourself. And you are afraid of tainting the essence of another, like me. [...] I know my identity and sense of self is wholly dependent and determined by my various relationships with others, from intimate personal relationships to my knowledge of who the president of the United States is. I essentially do not exist without others, so I embrace my dependency. Rugged individualism and the every-man's-an-island notion are capitalist ideals to produce selfish, greedy, unempathetic human beings. I don't think you are any of those things. I think you are more afraid of losing yourself, your identity (whatever that is). I, on the other hand, sometimes desire to loose myself completely and absorb into humanity as a pure concept of continuous expansion. And again, I think this is how we balance each other out. So for me, since I know and accept that I will forever be in an interdependent relationship with others, it becomes more an issue of choosing the right people to surround myself with. I have verbalized on several occasions the numerous and various reasons I have chosen you as a partner/lover so I will not bore you with tedious repetition. If after reading all this and you agree with what I'm saying, yet you still "don't believe in us," as you said on the phone, then I must not truly be the "right" person for you.

What I really think it comes down to is that you are gauging my worth by things outside of me (a Michael notion, which I have expressed on numerous occasions, but always before in terms of gauging one's own self-worth; yet it is also common for people to do this to others as well). You are gauging my worth to you, my worth as your lover or girlfriend by my plans for when I get released from prison: if I will be able to hold down a job and bring in an income, if I will be able to re-establish my art career, if my goals (which are things outside of me and don't define who I am) are realistic and practical. This is not only a notion that Michael challenges; it is also one that capitalism promotes because it helps to perpetuate the culture of endless want and dissatisfaction. If we align ourselves to Michael's notion that we, as human beings, all desire the same thing: to be loved and feel love. And if we also believe, as Michael says, that we are all perfect for the mere fact that we exist; and we strip away all the outside things like your perceived ability for me to achieve my goals/plans as well as my values and beliefs (because you are correct when you said that our shared values and beliefs is not enough to maintain our lovers status), then it comes down to love: how I love you and how you feel to be loved by me. How does my love feel to you? [...] If you search your heart and truly feel that the manner in which I love you does not fit your needs and desires, then you will have your answer. Because I will not compromise how I love, for anyone, even you my darling. I will always love expansively.

I know you are aware of my tendencies to fall into co-dependency because I have told you so. But now I feel you are using it (and also slightly, my honesty and my trust in you that you would understand and still accept me) against me. I am painfully aware that in the past I have lost myself in romantic relationships: I tend to forfeit my own personal goals, desires, and needs for that of my partners. I have even allowed myself to indulge in insane behaviors and crazed acts of a stereotypical possessive, co-dependent soon-to-be-exgirlfriend. But that was a very long time ago. And during my freshman year at college, knowing that I had this unexpansive tendency/history about me, I made a deal with this cosmic entity (I called Bob—don't ask, I was smoking a lot of weed and living alone in an off-campus apartment, isolating). I swore to forfeit all romantic and sexual relationships in order for my art career to flourish. So for three years (for the majority of my undergraduate years), I did not engage in any sexual activities nor any relationship remotely romantic; and indeed my art career did flourish. [...] I often fear that I cursed myself with that deal I made—I fear that I will never be able to have both a successful art career and lover/partner, simultaneously. And if you truly decide to not be my lover without really giving it a chance, then I will at least be one step closer to fulfilling that cursed prophecy. And I can only thank you for ending it before I get even more attached and involved—lessening the pain a bit.

[...] If you are happier now that you have released yourself from the "burden" of being my boyfriend (referenced from your letter written 12/4/08)—because you did sound much happier on the phone after coming to the conclusion that you are no longer in love with me—then I will not press the issue. Because who am I to deprive you of happiness. I am strong enough to endure temporary suffering for your long-term happiness (how dramatically martyrish does that sound? :)).

Well, I think I expressed everything I needed to—I will say no more. I am so sincerely sorry, for both of us, that you no longer believe in us. What a horrible loss.

Always with Love,
Jennifer Moon, R.P.

• • •

VSPW (Valley State Prison for Women), Chowchilla, CA

January 1, 2009

Dear Jonathan,

Happy New Year. I hope you had a good new year. Did you celebrate? I'm sure you did. Excuse my lackadaisical tone. I can't help it. I'm torn between wishing you all the happiness in the world because I love you and you deserve it; and then, on the other hand, I'm overcome by fear and the awful feelings of anxiety and sadness at the prospect of you sharing the new year with a new love interest. I know you said that there isn't another person: that isn't the reason you fell out of love with me. And I believe you. But it doesn't mean you could not have met someone or that you've been interested or attracted to someone in particular and now that you're free of me, you can act on it. I know that my indulgence into these types of insecure ramblings are highly unattractive. That is, at least, the primary message and #1 no-no in that one book, Why Men Love Bitches, which Monika was pushing on me. Now I'm thinking I should have read it because I can't help but partially think that my all-too-honest and seemingly constant verbalization of my insecurities and need for reassurance chased you away. Perhaps it is as you say, one's significant other doesn't need to know every thought that comes into one's head, especially if it is potentially hurtful (and in this case, it seemed to hurt me). I guess I do tend to take things (like the concept of complete openness and honesty at all times) too far. I take it to the extreme extreme where it's no longer about the original concept (ex: sincerity, openness, and honesty) and it becomes something else, which often has no resemblance to the original (like supreme insecurities run rampant). And I suppose this tendency of mine can fall in line with your concern that I am too fantasy-based. Or maybe I'm just a fucking human being and cannot always be expansive at every given moment, especially when living in a highly controlled and often uncomfortable and stressful environment. But whatever whatever... I'm not feeling that great (physically that is, my old bunkie got me sick with a sore throat and cough, which I'm constantly trying to suppress so my new roomies don't freak that I'm contaminating the room with my germs or think something's wrong with me like I'm weak, sickly, or unclean—isn't it sad that I've been reduced to these sorts of concerns?).

[…] A lot of people in here say this and perhaps it's just a coping mechanism, but I am starting to really believe that I needed to come here. No matter how much I fucking hate it here and how much I want to get the fuck out (and how much I blame it for our break up), I have to also admit that I am learning a lot about myself: my emotional patterns as well as my thought patterns. Doing my first year of sobriety in prison is like a double-whammy: I'm getting a double-dose lesson in powerlessness and acceptance as well as willingness. I hate that this seems to have been necessary for me; but having the most important thing to me, which is freedom, taken away has severely woken me up to the reality of my life (or lack of it for many years now). Whether you believe me or not (it doesn't really matter), I am more focused and determined than I have ever been since an undergrad; and I can see it grow everyday by the new patterns of actions I am continually developing each day, no matter how subtle or seemingly small. So even though I desperately wish I was not here or am sure that if I wasn't here we would still be lovers, I have accepted that this is a necessary chapter in my own personal journey. I will come out a stronger person in so many varying ways; and it saddens me to think you will not be there for me to share it with.

[…] Since we're on the subject of Naomi Klein, I may as well do my usual commentary on it. […]

I enjoyed the article, as always. Thank you. I don't think I want to read any of her books right now though. I need to concentrate on my own work. Plus, even though we may share similar goals, the manner in which we wish to implement revolutionary changes are vastly different. I am an artist and informed by an extensive art education. Naomi, whether she likes it or not, functions primarily in the realm of politics with a background in journalism. I think this is where her problems and frustrations lie. You know I don't believe in pop politics; and Klein eventually comes to this conclusion as well. As MacFarquhar writes, "It is clear, in 'The Shock Doctrine,' just how deeply she disdains the political." MacFarquhar continues by stating, "Klein believes that changes comes about only when social movements become so large and disruptive that politicians can no longer ignore them." You and I both agree that the revolution must begin with a cultural revolution; and that means focusing on and utilizing popular culture through music and art. MacFarquhar also writes, "For someone who places so much weight on social movements, though, Klein can get dyspeptic when she finds herself in the middle of one. Activists are so earnest, so dedicated, so—like her parents. 'Marches depress me,' she says." These blatant and un-self-critical forms of social movements are not interesting to me either. Perhaps there is a difference between social and cultural movements? Klein gets it a little bit when she says, "'Get out there and say some crazy stuff! And then, suddenly, it'll seem more reasonable for politicians to take riskier positions.'" This is similar to my interest in moving the realm of fantasy into current reality: it ups the ante or raises the bar to allow for new fantasies beyond our current imagination. It's all about allowing for continuous expansion. I actually think Naomi would like my work because "The only kind of protest she likes is the Yippie kind, theatrical enough to be entertaining and self mocking enough to dilute the earnestness..." I don't know about Yippie (I don't really know what that is or who that refers to), but my work is definitely theatrical and self-mocking or self-critical as well as political, revolutionary, and sincere.

And another difference is that Klein and her husband, Lewis (who interestingly enough in regards to us, "make a point of preserving their dependence upon each other"), have focused primarily on the negative, on what is wrong and what they are against. And they eventually realize this as well. MacFarquhar writes, "They are tired of being against things all the time..." This is something that is also stressed by Foucault in the preface of anti-oedipus, "prefer what is positive and multiple" and "Do not use...political action to discredit, as mere speculation, a line of thought. Use political practices as an intensifier of thought, and analysis as a multiplier of the forms and domains for the intervention of political action." Naomi also utilizes irony, which I think is ineffective and old ('"Naomi would use more irony, because we've gotten past our romanticism about how we change the world."'). And you know I'm a romantic. And lastly, Naomi "...refuses to say, 'Here's the alternative, here's what we all have to line up and fight for.'" You and I both know that we need to not only offer, but also have in place, an alternative to capitalism and other O&R systems.

Overall though, I think she's pretty great. Definitely someone we should work with. By the way, did you ever get a response from her research assistant about the Global Warming Jacket project? I'm glad you emailed her. I love that "...Klein celebrated the anarchic formlessness of the anti-corporate protests..." because you also know I celebrate formlessness. But the absolute best and most poignant point Klein makes is at the end of the article. MacFarquhar explains Klein's current theme, which Klein reiterates in all her numerous speaking engagements, in the following quote:

> Violent autocrats of the free-market persuasion, though there have been many, have not soiled Friedman's name in the way that Stalin soiled Marx; somehow, the misdeeds of a Pinochet or a Suharto or a Yeltsin are attributed to these men as individuals—to their lust for power, their greed, their drinking. But Klein holds capitalism guilty of all their sins.

So there are other things contained in the article that I can comment on, but unfortunately I don't have time. I only have 30 minutes until recall and lock down until dinner, and I want to get this letter out tonight (it's now Sunday, 01/04/09). If you can't already tell by my numerous typos, I rushed through my commentary of the article; so excuse me if my comments are not well-developed or thoroughly explained.

I think I have said everything that I wanted to and have responded to your last two letters in a satisfactory manner. This is usually the part of my letter where I tell you how much I love you and miss you and can't wait 'til the day we are once again reunited so that I can fuck you silly. But alas, that is no more. But whatever, I still love you, I still miss you, and I still cannot wait until the day I get to see you and give you a big hug.

Once again, always with love,

Jennifer Moon, R.P.

• • •

VSPW (Valley State Prison for Women), Chowchilla, CA

January 7, 2009

Dear Jonathan,

I received your letter of 12/21/08. At first, I didn't want to open it because the postmarked date on the envelope (12/22/08) corresponded to the week you decided you were no longer in love with me. I figured this must be the "Dear John" letter: the letter where you apologetically break my heart. But I eventually (and reluctantly) read it and was, once again, shocked at how quickly (it being reduced to days now) your feelings for me can change. This particular letter of yours wasn't gushing with love and adoration; but it was obvious you still loved me. And as with your last letter, it filled me with incredible sorrow and heartache to read words of love from you knowing you no longer feel this way.

[...] Now that I got the sad, depressing part out of the way, I will respond to your letter, which presented many interesting notions that need to be discussed further and more in depth. I wish I was out there with you because as a team, inspiring and working with one another, we could get so much more done. It is so incredibly frustrating to be in here when there is so much that needs to be done, so much I want to do. Sometimes I start panicking, feeling time ticking away and that things are happening out in the free world while I'm stuck, locked-up in here, not a part of anything. But soon I will have my day; and I need to focus and write and plan while I'm in here so that when I do get out, I can go straight into action. Getting letters like the one I just received from you definitely helps to motivate me and keep me focused. I am at least very grateful that you are still willing to communicate and interact with me on that level if nothing else.

[...] I just got off the phone with you (it's now Sunday, 01/11/09), and I'm left with this horrible feeling of being needy and pathetic. Perhaps it's not such a great idea for me to talk to you on the phone for a while. I truly aspire to be expansive no matter what personal issues I'm going through at the time; but when it comes to matters of the heart, I don't fair as well. I guess it comes down to acceptance (like with most things). And I'm having difficulty accepting your loss of love for me because I don't understand it. Perhaps you also don't understand it, which is why you are unsure about the form(s) our future relationship will take. I need to accept that it is not necessary for me to understand the reasons why in order to accept that it is over. I need to trust in continuous expansion: I need to trust that you were brought into my life to expand it, not to prove that I truly did curse myself into never finding/experiencing lasting love and a partner to share life. Perhaps your role is to simply be my Revolution Partner and nothing more. And I must be okay with that—I will be okay with it. I'm just mourning. Please understand that I'm doing the best I can. And if I occasionally have fallen into desperation mode, it's only because I'm allowing my feelings of hurt, pain, abandonment, loss, and confusion to control the things I say to you. As one of my roomies said, "I know it hurts like hell, but you need to trust that he was brought into your life for a good reason. Try to focus on the positive and know that if it's meant to be, then it will be. And if it's not, it will open you up for someone else who will love you the way you deserve to be loved. This is the time to focus on yourself and to know that you don't need him or anyone else, so that you can really learn to love yourself. But it doesn't mean it's not gonna hurt a lot."

The one thing I have learned here and absolutely love is the amazing amounts of kindness and compassion from the women here. On the one hand, a lot of the women are continually trying to cultivate this facade of hardness; and they're out there on the yard, in the mix, wheeling and dealing. But then, I am continually surprised by tremendous acts of sincere caring and kindness from relative strangers. And it's not just towards me. I witness it everyday amongst my fellow inmates. And this I think is rare amongst strangers out in the free world. I think there is an automatic bond that exists between all the women here (especially the ones you live with in close quarters). There is a special, unique form of love and an understanding because we are all in the same boat, so to speak. People look out for each other in here. There is more sharing that occurs in here than I have ever witnessed out in the free world. I have continually experienced people giving up half of what little they have so that their roommate will not go without basic essentials like, shampoo or a toothbrush or even coffee. I wish the general public out in the free world would also realize that we, as human beings under an O&R, power-driven system and paradigm, are also in the same boat. Free-world people can actually learn a lot from prisoners in this sense. [...] Now, I'm thinking how unfortunate it is that one must experience group tragedy before one can bond with strangers. I refuse to believe this is an innate human condition [...]. I believe ideas of separateness, individualism, otherness, and selfishness have been bred and cultivated and ingrained into society, culture, and people. And I believe it can be inspired out of them. And this is ultimately what we are working toward with the revolution. [...]

[...] It's now Saturday, March 7. It's now been two months since I've been sitting on this letter. My mom came to visit me last Saturday and informed me that you moved, which is why you didn't answer my last two attempts to call you. At first I was a little surprised that you had moved and not informed me with a letter. But then I had to remind myself that I hadn't written you either (though I've been working on this letter, which is now 16-pages long, off and on for two months). So I guess I can't be too "butt hurt," as they say here, that you ceased correspondence with me. [...] I still consider you my R.P. and my friend and I hope to continue working with you and expanding upon our friendship when I get out. I hope you feel the same.

Since you are my friend and I love you dearly, I feel I should inform you on what's been going on with me since we lasted talked two months ago. I hope you do the same with me. I hand wrote part of this letter a month ago and just haven't typed it out yet so I will do so now.

It's now Sunday, February 8th. I tried calling you yesterday, Saturday, morning around 8:15 am but you weren't home. I talked to my parents instead and asked my mom to call you to let you know that I was gonna try calling you this morning at 8:15 am; but they didn't let me out for my phone call (or else I was distracted and maybe they did open the door but I forgot or I didn't know what time it was). I really wanted to talk to you though. I would have preferred to talk to you directly and in real time rather than having to write this to you in a letter. As you can see from the date at the start of this letter, I've been sitting on this letter for over a month now. I want to finally send this letter off to you but in order to do so, I feel I also need to tell you that I am at a very different place than where I was a month ago. I don't want to mislead you to think that I am still pining away for you, for example. But one or, rather, two things are for certain, I will always love you, Jonathan, and I will always be R.P.'s with you (in fact, I'm counting on you being my revolution partner). But the most significant change that has recently occurred in my life (the day after my birthday in fact) is that I unexpectedly entered an intimate and romantic relationship with some-one: one of my roommates, in fact (the one I referenced on page 6 of this letter), and also the most amazing woman I have ever known. Her name is Beverly B. And I seriously think I'm falling in love. This may sound somewhat ridiculous to you or maybe even like an escape or consolation into a rebound relationship, but I can guarantee you that it is not (though I don't know why I feel the need to justify my relationship with Beverly to you, or my feelings: though I also know that even though you broke-up with me—you were the one to fall out of love with me—I know you still care about me and love me [as I also feel for you] and, therefore, I know you may also be concerned about my well-being in regards to this new relationship of mine). I will spare you the in depth details of our relationship, but I will tell you that I have never experienced such intense emotions as I have with Beverly. Perhaps it is what they say—it is because we are both women. When people here find out that this is my first romantic relationship with a woman, they all have the same response: "Oh, you're gonna fall in love." And sure as shit, I am falling in love. [...]

[...] So that's what I wrote a month ago. It's now Thursday, March 10th, and my love for Beverly, her love for me, and our relationship has only grown stronger and more committed. I know I may sound silly, blinded by a schoolgirl-type crush. But it really isn't and that's all I will say about it: I will not torture you more with my lovesick ramblings.

[...] I'm trying to parole back to Felicity House so I hope we can hang out and go to meetings when I get out, which is just over two months from now (71 days to be exact). I'm still very serious about the revolution so I hope you are too. [...] I love you, Jonathan, and I hope you still want to maintain and develop an intimate friendship with me.

With Deep Love, Respect, Admiration, and Adoration,
Jennifer Moon, R.P.

• • •

VSPW (Valley State Prison for Women), Chowchilla, CA

April 11, 2009

Dear Jonathan,

I haven't heard from you, especially since my last letter, so I thought I'd write you another short note to make sure you're doing okay. Hopefully what I disclosed towards the end of my last tome (a word I picked up from you) of a letter didn't turn you off from communicating with me—or worse, not desire a relationship with me. But you did stop communicating with me (or more specifically, writing me since I could no longer call you) long before you knew of my relationship with Beverly, so I don't think it's that. Hopefully, you are well and nothing is amiss in your life. I'd like to think that you are busy with school, music, your new living situation, etc., etc. and haven't had the time to write. If you could, perhaps you can drop me a quick note so that I know you are okay and that we are okay. Because I am paroling in 39 days and a wake-up and I'd like us to continue our relationship, especially as R.P.'s (because I am still dedicated and committed to the revolution as I'd like to believe you are as well). [...]

Everything is going well for me. I absolutely despise my job though, and the free staff who have fascistic, power-enamored, ego-driven tendencies are beginning to truly wear on me: my patience and acceptance. I'm having a hard time remaining silent. They already wrote me a 115 (which is for serious misconduct that can result in a loss of 30-90 days) because I missed one day of work because I wasn't feeling good. And in the 115, they wrote, "...there is nothing wrong with her, she just does not want to work." Even though the very day before, Tina (my boss) sent me home early from work because I threw up. Then they wrote, "...I/M Moon just wanted to go back to her room to continue typing her 'Manifest' for the revolution she is planning." Can you believe they actually wrote that in the 115?! I think they were trying to make me appear crazy. Though I laughed out loud when I read it. [...] Luckily when I was heard on my 115, the lieutenant was super cool and dropped it down to a 128 (I didn't loose any days). He didn't even read the 115. He only read the first sentence, which was good because the warehouse fucks were trying hard to make me sound bad. And then this past Friday, Kathy wrote me a 128 for singing "Somewhere Over the Rainbow" in the office as I was coming into work. And then today (Tuesday, 4/13), all the critical workers who had to work yesterday during generator testing (which is unfortunately me) got a 128-B because the C.O.'s found a packet of about 20 cool-aides on the ground at work change where we strip out. Someone was trying to smuggle them in and since no one would cop to it, we all got a write-up. I have to be very careful now though because I think three related 128's is an automatic 115. Oh but the good news is that I got a new face sheet and they recalculated my days and it seems like I'm going home a day early, on 5/19 instead of 5/20.

I want to get this letter to you so I'm gonna end this here. Sorry it's short and complainy. I really hope you are happy and doing well. I miss you and think of you often. Can't wait to see you when I get out.

With Love, Wishes of Happiness, and Thoughts of Revolution,
Jennifer Moon, R.P.

• • •

About the Author

Jennifer Moon is a Los Angeles based artist, adventurer, and revolutionary. Her life is propelled by fervent courage, unadulterated love, unfaltering faith, and a resolute refusal to live a life based in any form of fear. For more information about Jennifer Moon and her practice, visit jmoon.net.

www.ingramcontent.com/pod-product-compliance
Lightning Source LLC
LaVergne TN
LVHW052304100826
845147LV00006B/669

9781300586791